John Sarich at

Chateau Ste. Michelle

Canoe Ridge Estate Vineyard

John Sarich at Chateau Ste. Michelle

FOR COOKS
WHO LOVE WINE

JOHN SARICH

WITH LORI MCKEAN

SASQUATCH BOOKS
SEATTLE

To my boys,
Biagio and Dominic,
my strictest critics and
my greatest love

John Sarich at Chateau Ste. Michelle
Copyright © 1997 by John Sarich and Stimson Lane Vineyards & Estates, Ltd.

Distributed in Canada by Raincoast Books Ltd.

Author: John Sarich
Editor: Barry Provorse
Copy editor: Judy Gouldthorpe
Cover and interior design: TeamDesign
Photographer: Darrell Peterson
Project director — concept: Robin Struyvenberg
Project director — content: Katie Sims
Produced by: Documentary Book Publishers

Library of Congress Cataloging-in-Publication Data

LC# 97-22422

Sarich, John
John Sarich at Chateau Ste. Michelle

ISBN 1-57061-121-1

1. Cookbook, 2. Recipes, 3. Wine, 4. Pacific Northwest

Sasquatch Books
615 Second Avenue
Seattle, Washington 98104
books@sasquatchbooks.com
(206) 467-4300
http://www.sasquatchbooks.com

Sasquatch Books publishes high-quality cookbooks, exceptional travel books, nonfiction
and children's books related to the Pacific Northwest. Through its subsidiary,
Documentary Book Publishers, Sasquatch publishes books for corporate and institutional
clients across North America. For more information about our titles and services, contact
us at the address listed above, or view our site on the World Wide Web.

Printed in Canada

Table of Contents

Introduction
page 6

White Wine Menus
page 14

Weekdays
page 18

Weekends
page 50

Celebrations
page 68

Red Wine Menus
page 82

Weekdays
page 86

Weekends
page 110

Celebrations
page 156

Stocks and Sauces
page 166

Guide to Food and Wine Pairing
page 170

Index
page 172

Introduction

HIS IS A BOOK FOR COOKS WHO LOVE WINE. Its menu-based presentation is meant to answer the questions I face every day. I've always done the cooking for my family and, like many others, I come home at night faced with that perennial dilemma, "What should we have for dinner?" If I have a taste for something special, and time enough to prepare it, the next question is, "What will go with it?" And after making the effort to fix a nice meal, I want to celebrate it with a glass of good wine, one that complements the flavors of the meal.

As culinary director for Chateau Ste. Michelle, I spend my days presenting food and wine to some of the best-known chefs and food and wine writers in the world. So for me, meal planning and cooking are a way of life. This book is the outcome of my experience at the winery, in the restaurant business and at home. The menu suggestions combine some of my favorite fresh-flavored foods, light sauces and fine wines.

Cooking and wine have been a major part of my life from the beginning. I was raised on the spirited Mediterranean cooking and homemade wines of my parents and grandparents, who settled in Seattle after immigrating from the Dalmatian coast of Croatia. They brought with them a delight in all things edible, which, combined with their zest for life and their enjoyment of good company, established a deep and permanent affinity for sharing the pleasures of the table.

As far back as I can remember, my family's home meals always had an air of celebration. The Sunday dinners at my grandparents' house were family feasts, where relatives and friends gathered to share lively conversation, homemade wines and succulent food. Indeed, Grandpa's fragrant lamb is my earliest recollection of the sheer delight of eating. He cooked his garlic-studded lamb all day over an outdoor spit, basting it with thick green olive oil and fresh rosemary under the admiring scrutiny of his hungry guests. Inside the house, the kitchen was filled with chatter and delectable aromas as Grandma and my mom, sister and aunts turned out

Sarich family gatherings

mostaccioli, dishes made with sauerkraut and stewed ham hocks, delicious salads and freshly baked desserts that defy description. The food was never served in courses at these meals but set out on the table all at once for everyone to enjoy.

A highlight of those Sunday dinners was Grandpa's homemade wine. At big celebrations, my dad, my brother and I would proudly follow Grandpa down the basement stairs and help him crack open a new barrel. My mouth still waters as I recall the heady smell of prosciutto and salami hanging there to cure among the oak barrels and fermenting wine. After decanting his spicy beverage, we'd carry the jugs upstairs and distribute them around the table. Grandpa didn't know it at the time, but the grapes he purchased from California to make his wine were a variety of the same Zinfandel grapes that were raised in his native Croatia.

As you can tell, my love affair with food and wine goes back a long, long way. But it wasn't until I was stationed in Vietnam as a 19-year-old communications specialist, traveling throughout Southeast Asia and the Far East, that I realized I was far more interested in the food people served than in seeing the sights. A tour of Hong Kong was a watershed for me. The foods and customs were so utterly different from anything I'd ever experienced back home that I might as well have arrived on another planet. I was fascinated with the people — what they ate, how they ate, what they drank, how they conversed at mealtimes — and thus began an ongoing curiosity about different cultures and cuisines that has not abated in all my travels around the world. Since then, travel has been the source of my food and wine education.

After finishing a degree at Seattle University, something happened out of the blue that changed the course of my life. By sheer luck I happened to attend a celebration commemorating Chateau Ste. Michelle's move to its 87 acre Woodinville facilities, built on the impeccably landscaped grounds of lumber baron Frederick Stimson's summer home. Intrigued and curious about what I saw, I thought working at the winery might be a great way to learn and earn with a summer job, and I eagerly filled an open slot at the winery as a wine tour guide — just to get in the door.

My enthusiasm for food and wine didn't go unnoticed for long, and when I suggested cooking demonstrations as part of the winery's promotional events, I was invited to teach the class. My kitchen skills were based on years of home study. I was an intuitive cook with no formal training, but I loved food and wine, and for me this was the beginning of a very satisfying career.

The winery and that job expanded. I became Chateau Ste. Michelle's regional representative, using my skills in cooking to present Chateau Ste. Michelle wines, and was transferred to San Francisco. There, I met chefs from Sam's Bar and Grill, Fleur de Lis, Stanford Court and most of the city's other great restaurants. I also called on chefs up and down the Pacific Coast. Chateau Ste. Michelle was one of the first wineries in the country to offer more than wine list suggestions. We consulted on menus — food and wine planning.

I was always drawn to cooking, and in 1980 I could no longer resist the temptation to put my well-tempered food and wine experience to the practical test. I co-founded Seattle's acclaimed Adriatica Restaurant, which specialized in Mediterranean-style cuisine. Later, I opened the Dalmacija Ristoran in Seattle's Pike Place Market, where Croatian and Dalmatian fare were the dominants. The restaurants were challenging and successful, but I missed the winery. So when Chateau Ste. Michelle invited me to start up a comprehensive wine and food program for them, I jumped at the chance, returning to the company as culinary director in 1990.

During my absence, Chateau Ste. Michelle had grown in stature and holdings. Today, Chateau Ste. Michelle owns 1,280 acres of Columbia Valley vineyards, embracing such single vineyard designations as Cold Creek and Canoe Ridge Estate, each with its own distinct micro-climate. Our grapes are raised in the Columbia Valley, and under the direct supervision of our winemaker, Mike Januik, our red wines are fermented and aged at our Canoe Ridge Estate Winery, overlooking the Columbia River. Our white wines are fermented and barrel-aged here at the Woodinville winery. Prestigious national and international awards proudly grace our halls.

JOINING WINE WITH FOOD

A T CHATEAU STE. MICHELLE I'm able to share my enthusiasm for wine and food with consumers every day. At the winery, I conduct wine and food tastings, cooking classes and special dinners. I often supervise elaborate events, all designed to further people's enjoyment of food and wine. Many of these events are held in the winery's manor house, which is on the National Register of Historic Places.

Much of the time I am on the road, preparing meals and presenting seminars and classes for wine and food professionals and aficionados around the world. These culinary tours have taken me from cooking demonstrations at the Disney Institute in Florida to the Culinary Institute of America and the James Beard House in New York to top restaurants and hotels in Singapore, Bangkok, Hawaii and Europe. I recently traveled to the famed Sandy Lane Resort on Barbados, where I presented flavors of the Pacific Northwest, including several varietal wines paired with Olympia oysters, fresh halibut and Columbia River caviar.

One of my greatest pleasures is cooking with, and for, some of the most celebrated chefs in the world: Julia Child, Hawaii's treasure Alan Wong, European master chef Georges Blanc, the chefs of the Ritz-Carlton Hotels, and other fine chefs closer to my Pacific Northwest home.

Those of you who have read my first cookbook, *Food & Wine of the Pacific Northwest*, or who have watched *Taste of the Northwest*, my television cooking show, are already familiar with my style of cooking. While I strive for simplicity (a goal by no means as simple as it sounds), I love foods with bold, vibrant, distinct flavors. My mission is to showcase the natural flavor of foods by concentrating on the ingredients and letting them do the work in combination with the herbs, sauces and marinades that underscore what nature has already accomplished so well. The wine I pour is, naturally, the ultimate complement to the meal.

THE WHY OF NORTHWEST FLAVORS

W E WHO LIVE in the Pacific Northwest are blessed with an abundance of farm-fresh fruits and vegetables, wild berries and game, poultry and meats of all varieties, superb seafood and superlative dairy products — just for openers. Most of our fish is fresh from the sea. Beef raised here is grain fed rather than corn fattened, which gives it a different flavor. The vine fruits of the Pacific Northwest are sweet and succulent. Along with a few possessions, my grandpa brought a fig tree from the old country and planted it in Seattle, where it still produced wonderful, succulent fruit each season.

And then there are our wines. All too few regions in the world have just the right combination of soils and micro-climates for producing truly significant vintages. The Columbia Valley of Eastern Washington, where Chateau Ste. Michelle has spent over 40 years growing fine grape varietals, is one of them.

Carved out by ancient glaciers, lava flows and extensive floods, the Columbia Valley has buckled and folded over the eons, resulting in a series of high ridges that traverse the valley from east to west. This dramatic basin occupies the same northerly latitudes as the great wine-growing regions of Bordeaux and Burgundy in France. Tucked within its folded slopes are many singular vineyard sites, each with its own uniquely individual soil, altitude, exposure and climate. Wherever these natural elements combine perfectly, the grapes, and ultimately the wines, exhibit special aromas, flavors and textures, a condition the French call *terroir* — the taste of the soil.

The Columbia Valley is protected from moist Pacific air by the Cascade Range, and its average rainfall of under eight inches a year allows our grape growers with irrigation to control the watering of their vines. Warm, sunny days and extra-long daylight hours during the growing season ensure sweet, fully ripened fruit, which translates into intense varietal flavors in the end product. Cool nights preserve those crisp acids in the wines that keep the palate refreshed. Varietals that do exceptionally well in this region include classic whites such as Riesling, Sauvignon Blanc, Semillon and Chardonnay. Columbia Valley reds, including Merlot, Cabernet Sauvignon, Syrah and Cabernet Franc, are packed with complex ripe fruit flavors and spicy aroma. And to the south, Oregon's temperate Willamette Valley is now world renowned for its outstanding Pinot Noir and Pinot Gris wines.

Finally, when I cook at home, I usually pour one or two wines with dinner. So with each menu, I've recommended those wines that I feel best suit the menu.

The Dynamics of Wine and Food

WINE IS OFTEN CALLED "nature's perfect condiment," and when matched with the right foods, it clears and refreshes the palate. Our taste buds perceive certain flavors and textures in foods, such as salt, sugar, acid, fat and bitterness, along with the sugar, acid, fruit, tannin and alcohol in wines. When wine meets food on our palates, all these components combine to create many different taste sensations. And while there are no absolute rules regarding the matching process, there are definite reasons why some wines taste better with certain foods. Varietal differences in wine are as important a consideration as the herbs and spices used in cooking the dish.

Wine can echo or enhance the flavors and textures of a dish. A satiny Merlot brimming with ripe cherry flavors will magnify the richness and texture of roast duck with cherry sauce, for example. It can also provide a contrast to flavors in the food and a palate-cleansing effect with rich or spicy dishes. A cucumber-crisp Sauvignon Blanc will slice right through the luxuriance of plump, briny oysters, and the potent tannins in a full-bodied Cabernet Sauvignon will prime the palate between bites of rare prime rib. And wine adds flavors to a dish. When serving salmon, you might pour an earthy Pinot Noir that carries the overtones of wild mushrooms and truffles. Or you could sharpen the smoothness of a simple roast chicken with the tropical fruit and buttery richness of a barrel-fermented Chardonnay.

In the best of pairings, wine and food interact perfectly on the palate. The acids and fruit flavor of a Semillon or Sauvignon Blanc will cleanse the palate and cool the heat of a spicy Asian shrimp dish, while at the same time the fruit flavors of the wine will complement the sweet sea taste of the shrimp. The sweetness of tender lamb can be leavened by the texture and fruit of a full-bodied Merlot, whereas the tannins in the wine mellow the richness of the meat.

Strongly flavored foods can overpower the delicacy of some wines. A robust steak needs to be matched with an equally hearty wine — a Cabernet or a Merlot, for example — to achieve balance on the palate. But that same red wine will curdle the proteins of the dairy product you choose for dessert. Your salmon won't appreciate that Cabernet either, but it will surely welcome a softer, subtler Pinot Noir or Merlot.

Given all of the above, the most important rule to remember is elemental. Simply put: drink the wine you prefer with the food you like best. What's important is your own taste and enjoyment. I offer these menus and recipes only as guidelines based on my own experience in matching wine with food. By all means try these recommendations, but experiment with wine and food pairings of your own.

Good Cooking

I'VE DIVIDED THE TEXT into two sections — White Wine Foods and Red Wine Foods. Each section has been subdivided into weekday menus, which either are quick to fix or can be prepared well in advance of company; weekend menus, which are a bit more complex; and celebration menus, for full-flavored feasts. I have also included several vegetarian menu suggestions. I don't always make dessert. Some menus have them and others don't. For the fastidious who like to start a dish from scratch, there's a separate chapter on stocks and sauces.

Once you've decided on a menu, read through the recipes thoroughly before making out your shopping list. Recipes are intended only as guidelines, and if you can't locate a certain ingredient, or if you prefer a different herb, don't be afraid to substitute.

All great dishes begin with fine ingredients, so take time at the market to select the highest-quality products you can find. Learn to use all your senses to gauge and assess the foods. Look for what Japanese chefs refer to as *Umami* — the essence of being — food so alive it seems to touch you back. Look at the color and luster of fruits and vegetables, weigh them in your hand. Every food has its own special character. Vine-ripened tomatoes glow with color and feel heavy in the hand. Fresh fish glistens and smells of the sea. Just-picked asparagus snaps apart sharply and runs with sweet juices. Seeking out high-quality ingredients takes only a few extra minutes, but it makes all the difference in the finished dish.

Back home, read through the recipes again to make sure you have a sound understanding of each step involved. Then do what professional chefs do: prepare all the items you're going to need one at a time. If a recipe calls for two cups of chopped tomatoes, chop them ahead of time and set them aside in a little bowl; get all your ingredients lined up in the same way before you start cooking. This initial organization will prevent frustration later on and greatly add to your enjoyment in preparing the meal.

Make the Meal an Occasion

*A*S I LEARNED from my own family gatherings, sitting down to a meal is much more than just eating. Mealtimes are occasions for relaxed talk, for sharing yourself with your family and showing your warm concern for them and the circle of friends gathered at the table. In so doing, you are nurturing those basic elements of social behavior that bind us all together. And certainly, enjoying wine with a meal is a simple way to celebrate life every single day. I hope you'll join me in that daily ceremony and perhaps begin it with the same old Croatian family toast that we use at every meal. *"Zevio!"* Grandpa would say, which means simply "To Life."

John Sarich
Culinary Director, Chateau Ste. Michelle

White Wine Foods

My appreciation of white wines came as an epiphany during my military service in Asia. There, where both the climate and food were hot, nothing was more satisfying with Asian flavors than a well-chilled Riesling. Since then, I have learned to cook with and serve white wines as varied in character as Dry Riesling and oak-aged Chardonnay.

Generally, white wines are described as either light and delicate or bold and full-bodied. Delicate Riesling, Gewurztraminer and Chenin Blanc have the natural crisp flavors of fresh fruit. They are always refreshing. Gewurztraminer and Johannisberg Riesling have a hint of sweetness, whereas others, such as Dry Riesling, leave only a slight impression of fresh fruit. These varietals are typically paired with veal, pork, chicken and turkey.

Semillon and Pinot Gris are considered lighter and more delicate white wines whereas Sauvignon Blanc and Chardonnay are generally considered full-bodied white wines. Their flavors and aromas are more complex than those of light white wines. They are usually rich with ripe fruit flavors and spicelike aromas. Semillon and Pinot Gris are best paired with the subtle flavors of shellfish and other seafood, while Sauvignon Blanc and Chardonnay are suited to more full-flavored seafood and poultry dishes.

White Wine Menus

WEEKDAYS

The Ultimate Baked Onion
Suggested Wine
Chardonnay
page 18

Grilled Marinated Pork Chops
Suggested Wine
Johannisberg Riesling
page 22

Calamari Fritti with Garlic Sauce
Suggested Wine
Sauvignon Blanc
page 26

Hazelnut Chicken Breasts with Dijon Yogurt Sauce
Suggested Wine
Chardonnay
page 30

Italian Pounded Chicken
Suggested Wine
Pinot Gris
page 34

Dalmatian Coast Dinner
Suggested Wine
Sauvignon Blanc
or
Dry Riesling
page 38

One–Dish Meals and Croatian Potato Bread
page 42

WEEKENDS

FRESH SPRING HALIBUT PROVENÇAL
Suggested Wine
Sauvignon Blanc
page 50

MAPLE–GLAZED SALMON WITH
PEACH AND PAPAYA CHUTNEY
Suggested Wine
Chardonnay
page 56

VEAL LOIN WITH SWEET PEPPER PURÉE
Suggested Wine
Chardonnay
page 62

CELEBRATIONS

CHINESE BARBECUED PORK CELEBRATION
Suggested Wine
Dry Riesling
or
Semillon
page 68

APPLE AND PRUNE STUFFED PORK TENDERLOIN
Suggested Wine
Sauvignon Blanc
or
Johannisberg Riesling
page 74

Basil Prawn and Feta Pasta

The Ultimate Baked Onion

I don't know what I like more about this dish, the aroma of baking onions or the rich flavors of Arborio rice, wild mushrooms, fennel and garlic when I bite into one. I'm glad I don't have to choose.

CABBAGE AND CRANBERRY SALAD
page 19

THE ULTIMATE BAKED ONION
page 20

SQUASH STICKS
page 21

Suggested Wine
Chardonnay

CABBAGE AND CRANBERRY SALAD

Serves 4

2 tablespoons pure olive oil

1 head green cabbage, grated or thinly sliced

1 yellow onion, thinly sliced

1½ cups fresh cranberries

1 clove

2 tablespoons white wine vinegar

2 tablespoons sugar

Salt

Heat skillet over medium-high heat then add olive oil. Add cabbage and onion and sauté for 5 minutes, stirring constantly. Add the cranberries and clove and reduce heat to low. Cover and simmer 5 minutes. Turn off heat. In a small bowl, whisk together vinegar and sugar until well blended. Salt to taste. Pour vinegar over warm cabbage and toss. Serve warm.

Wine Note

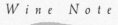

CHARDONNAY

BEST KNOWN AS THE POWER BEHIND THE GREAT WHITE BURGUNDIES OF FRANCE, THIS NOBLE GRAPE IS WIDELY GROWN THROUGHOUT THE NORTHWEST. CHARDONNAY'S FLAVORS RANGE FROM APPLE TO TROPICAL FRUITS TO EARTHY MINERALS — BEAUTIFULLY ENHANCED BY THE TOASTY, NUTTY BUTTERSCOTCH AND SPICE FLAVORS IMPARTED BY OAK AGING. ELEGANT AND FLAVORFUL, CHARDONNAY IS CURRENTLY THE WORLD'S HOTTEST–SELLING VARIETAL WINE.

THE ULTIMATE BAKED ONION

Serves 4

This dish makes a delicious companion for salmon or chicken. One year at our annual Northwest Wine Auction dinner, I served these onions as an accompaniment to poached king salmon set in a pool of beurre blanc.

4 large onions

2 tablespoons olive oil

Reserved onion centers, chopped

1 fennel bulb, finely diced

1 red bell pepper, finely diced

1 teaspoon dry mustard

2 garlic cloves, minced

2 tablespoons dry white wine

4 – 6 cups chicken stock, as needed (see page 167)

1¹/2 cups Arborio rice or short-grain white rice

¹/2 tablespoon chopped fresh thyme

1 tablespoon chopped fresh Italian parsley

Salt to taste

1 tablespoon butter

1 pound fresh chanterelles or other edible wild mushrooms, sliced

¹/2 cup freshly grated Parmesan cheese

Preheat oven to 350°F. Peel the onions and slice each one in half horizontally. Trim the bottoms so the onions sit flat. Scoop out the center portion of each onion half and reserve. Set the onions in a baking pan and fill the pan with ¹/2 inch of water. Cover the pan and bake the onions for 20 minutes, or until tender. Remove the onions from the pan and set aside to cool.

Meanwhile, heat the olive oil in a large, heavy saucepan over medium-high heat. When the oil is hot, stir in the chopped onions, fennel, red pepper, dry mustard and garlic. Cook, stirring often, until the vegetables are very soft, about 10 minutes. Stir in the wine and 1 cup of the chicken stock. Simmer the mixture for 3 minutes. Add the rice, stirring well, until the liquid is absorbed. Add 1 cup stock and continue stirring until the liquid is absorbed. Continue adding stock, 1 cup at a time, until the rice softens but still retains a slight firmness. Remove from the heat. Fold in the thyme, parsley and salt.

Heat the butter in a small skillet over medium-high heat. Add the mushrooms and cook quickly until softened, 3 to 5 minutes. Stir the mushrooms into the rice. Stuff the onions with the rice mixture, packing firmly and mounding in a dome over the top of the onion. Place the stuffed onions in a baking pan and pour 1¹/2 cups chicken stock around and over the onions (add water or white wine to stock if necessary to get enough liquid). Cover the onions and bake for 20 minutes, or until heated through. Top with grated Parmesan cheese.

Squash Sticks

Serves 4

1 tablespoon butter

1 tablespoon olive oil

2 small zucchini, cut into thin, matchlike sticks (julienne)

1 small yellow squash, cut into thin, matchlike sticks

2 medium carrots, peeled and cut into thin, matchlike sticks

1 yellow onion, peeled and cut into thin, matchlike sticks

1 red bell pepper, seeded and cut into thin, matchlike sticks

2 garlic cloves, minced

2 tablespoons dry white wine

1 tablespoon chopped fresh Italian parsley

1 teaspoon chopped fresh thyme

Salt and freshly ground black pepper to taste

Heat the butter and olive oil over high heat in a large skillet or wok. When sizzling, stir in the zucchini, yellow squash, carrots, onions, red pepper and garlic. Cook quickly, stirring constantly, for 3 minutes. Add the wine, parsley and thyme. Simmer 2 to 3 more minutes. Season with salt and pepper.

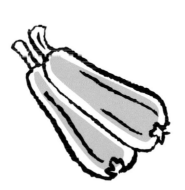

Grilled Marinated Pork Chops

On warm summer evenings, I often teach cooking classes
beside Chateau Ste. Michelle's herb garden, where parsley,
cilantro and oregano are picked fresh for this herb-lime pork
marinade. Along with spicy rice and black bean
salad and a well-dressed Riesling-poached apple, this
a favorite summertime meal.

SPICY RICE AND BLACK BEAN SALAD
page 23

GRILLED MARINATED PORK CHOPS
page 24

POACHED APPLES WITH
CARAMEL NUT TOPPING
page 25

Suggested Wines
Johannisberg Riesling
Late Harvest White Riesling

SPICY RICE AND BLACK BEAN SALAD

Serves 4 to 6

*If you're short of time, use canned black beans from your local market.
This quick and healthy salad can be prepared ahead and chilled overnight.*

2   cups cold cooked white rice

2   cups cooked black beans, drained

1   red onion, diced

1   bunch green onions, sliced

1   garlic clove, minced

1/8 teaspoon chili powder

1/8 teaspoon ground cumin

2   tablespoons chopped fresh cilantro

1/2 cup prepared red salsa, mild to hot,
    depending on taste

1   4-ounce can diced green chilies,
    drained

Place all ingredients together in a large bowl and toss. Allow mixture to sit at least 15 minutes before serving.

Wine Note

RIESLING

ONE OF THE WORLD'S MOST NOBLE GRAPES, THIS ANCIENT GERMANIC VARIETY
WAS AMONG THE FIRST VINES PLANTED IN THE NORTHWEST, AND THE WINE IS
MADE IN A VARIETY OF STYLES HERE. TYPICALLY, WASHINGTON RIESLINGS ARE
DELICATELY SPICED, WITH A PERFECT BALANCE OF CRISP ACID AND LUSCIOUS
STONE FRUIT FLAVORS. JOHANNISBERG RIESLING, ALSO CALLED WHITE RIESLING,
IS AN OFF–DRY — OR SLIGHTLY SWEET — WINE. SERVED CHILLED, THESE ZESTY
WINES ARE DELIGHTFULLY REFRESHING AS AN APERITIF AND MAKE OUTSTANDING
PARTNERS FOR SPICY FOODS. DRY RIESLINGS, WITH THE BAREST HINT OF SWEET-
NESS, ARE BECOMING INCREASINGLY POPULAR. THESE ELEGANT, SOPHISTICATED
WINES HAVE TANGY ACIDS AND COMPLEX LAYERS OF FRUIT AND SPICE, MAKING
THEM EXCEPTIONAL AS FOOD WINES OR SPLENDID FOR JUST SIPPING. THE RIESLING
GRAPE ALSO PROVIDES THOSE EXTRAORDINARY LATE–HARVEST DESSERT WINES
NOTED FOR HONEY–SWEET FRUIT FLAVORS.

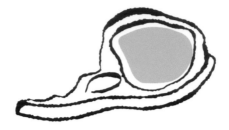

GRILLED MARINATED PORK CHOPS

Serves 4

2 tablespoons olive oil

Juice of two limes

2 tablespoons Chenin Blanc or other dry white wine

3 garlic cloves, minced

1 tablespoon chopped fresh cilantro

1 tablespoon chopped fresh parsley

1/2 tablespoon chopped fresh oregano

1 teaspoon chili powder

Pinch of red pepper flakes (optional)

Salt and freshly ground black pepper to taste

4 pork loin chops, 1/2 inch thick

In a large nonreactive mixing bowl, whisk together the olive oil, lime juice, wine, garlic, cilantro, parsley, oregano, chili powder, pepper flakes, salt and pepper. Rub each chop thoroughly with the marinade and place back in the bowl. Cover and chill for 1 to 2 hours.

Meanwhile, heat a charcoal grill or stove-top grill until hot. Grill the chops over high heat approximately 7 minutes on each side, to an internal temperature of 160°F.

POACHED APPLES WITH
CARAMEL NUT TOPPING

Serves 6

This is a dessert and wine combination that I served at a special dinner for the U.S. Congress to give them a taste of the Pacific Northwest. Poached apples can be prepared a day ahead of serving.

3 large Winesap or Rome Beauty apples, peeled, halved and cored

1 cup Johannisberg Riesling

1 clove

2 2-inch long slices orange zest

Preheat oven to 375°F. Place the apples in a nonreactive baking pan. Add the wine, clove and orange zest. Cover and bake for 15 minutes. Turn the apples and bake for another 15 minutes, or until tender when pierced with a fork. Remove the apples from the liquid and cool to room temperature.

CARAMEL NUT TOPPING

2 cups cold water

1/2 cup brown sugar, firmly packed

2 tablespoons sugar

1 teaspoon grated orange zest

3 tablespoons butter

1/2 cup chopped toasted walnuts or hazelnuts (see page 103)

1 cup whipping cream, whipped and lightly sweetened

Mix the water, brown sugar, sugar, orange zest and butter in a heavy saucepan. Bring to a boil over high heat, stirring constantly. Reduce heat and simmer rapidly until the mixture thickens, about 10 minutes. Remove the caramel sauce from the heat and stir in the chopped toasted nuts.

To serve, bring the apples to room temperature. Place each apple half, core side up, on a dessert plate. Fill each apple with hot Caramel Nut Topping and top with a dollop of whipped cream. Serve immediately.

Suggested Wine
Late Harvest White Riesling

Calamari Fritti with Garlic Sauce

When I opened Adriatica Restaurant, I wanted to serve really great fried calamari. After some research and many experiments, I developed this recipe, which became one of the restaurant's signature dishes. It's perfect with a light salad and pasta.

BIBB LETTUCE AND DIJON SALAD
page 27

CALAMARI FRITTI WITH GARLIC SAUCE
page 28

BASIL PRAWN AND FETA PASTA
page 29

Suggested Wine
Sauvignon Blanc

BIBB LETTUCE AND DIJON SALAD

Serves 4

2 heads Bibb lettuce

Juice of 1/2 lemon

2 tablespoons extra-virgin olive oil

1 teaspoon Dijon mustard

Pinch of salt

Pinch of white pepper

Wash and separate leaves of Bibb lettuce and place in a chilled bowl. In a small bowl, combine the lemon juice, olive oil, Dijon mustard, salt and white pepper. Mix well. Pour over lettuce and toss before serving.

Chef's Tip

PREPARING SQUID

SOAK THE CLEANED SQUID IN ICE WATER BEFORE COATING WITH FLOUR. THIS PREVENTS IT FROM OVERCOOKING AND HELPS THE FLOUR ADHERE TO THE SURFACE. BECAUSE PEANUT OIL CAN BE HEATED TO HIGHER TEMPERATURES THAN OTHER COOKING OILS, IT IS BEST FOR FRYING CALAMARI.

BUYING AND COOKING SQUID

LOOK FOR SQUID, ALSO KNOWN AS CALAMARI, WITH BRIGHT, SHINY SKIN THAT SMELLS FRESH LIKE THE SEA. SQUID COOKS VERY QUICKLY, BECOMING TOUGH WHEN OVERCOOKED. TO PREVENT OVERCOOKING, TEST REPEATEDLY WHILE COOKING AND REMOVE THE SQUID FROM THE HEAT THE INSTANT IT IS DONE. TWO POUNDS OF WHOLE SQUID WILL YIELD ONE AND A HALF POUNDS OF CLEANED SQUID. SQUID MEAT IS VERY LEAN AND VERY HIGH IN PROTEIN.

CALAMARI FRITTI WITH GARLIC SAUCE

Serves 4 as an appetizer

1 1/2 pounds squid (5 to 8 inches long), cleaned and cut into 1-inch rings, reserving tentacles, or 1 pound frozen squid rings and tentacles, thawed

Ice water for soaking

3/4 cup peanut oil

2 cups flour

1 teaspoon paprika

1/4 teaspoon ground white pepper

1/4 teaspoon salt

Lemon wedges

Soak the squid rings in ice water for 5 to 10 minutes. Meanwhile, heat the oil in a deep, heavy-bottomed saucepan over medium-high heat, just until smoking. Mix together the flour, paprika, white pepper and salt. Lift each piece of squid from the ice water and shake to remove excess water. Dip the squid in the seasoned flour and shake to remove excess flour. Fry squid in the hot oil until golden brown, about 2 minutes. Serve with lemon wedges and Garlic Sauce.

GARLIC SAUCE

1 loaf day-old French bread, crust trimmed, cut into 1-inch cubes

4 teaspoons white wine vinegar

2 teaspoons water

4 garlic cloves, minced

1 cup olive oil

2 tablespoons finely chopped fresh basil

1 tablespoon finely chopped fresh Italian parsley

Salt and freshly ground black pepper

In a mixing bowl, combine the bread cubes, vinegar, water and garlic. Mash with a fork to form a thick paste. Whisk in the olive oil, one tablespoon at a time, mixing thoroughly. Stir in the basil, parsley, salt and pepper to taste. Serve at room temperature.

BASIL PRAWN AND FETA PASTA

Serves 4

2 tablespoons olive oil

1 yellow onion, diced

3 garlic cloves, minced

1 pound prawns, peeled and deveined

1/4 cup Sauvignon Blanc or other dry
   white wine

Juice of 1/4 lemon

5 Roma tomatoes, peeled and diced

1/4 cup chopped fresh basil

2 tablespoons chopped fresh parsley

Pinch of red pepper flakes

1/2 cup crumbled feta cheese

12 ounces linguine, cooked al dente

Heat the olive oil in a skillet over medium-high heat. Briskly sauté the onion until softened, about 3 minutes. Add the garlic and prawns and cook just until prawns turn a bright orange color, about 5 minutes. Add the wine, lemon juice and diced tomatoes, mixing thoroughly. When tomatoes have softened, add the basil, parsley and red pepper flakes. Cook for 2 minutes, then fold in the feta cheese. Heat until the cheese has softened. Ladle the sauce over the prepared linguine.

Chef's Tip

PERFECTLY COOKED PASTA — AL DENTE

ONCE YOU'VE ADDED DRIED PASTA TO BOILING WATER AND IT HAS SOFTENED, THERE'S A SIMPLE TEST FOR TELLING WHEN THE PASTA IS PERFECTLY COOKED. PULL A STRAND FROM THE POT AND BITE INTO IT: THERE SHOULD BE A MINUSCULE "EYE" IN THE CENTER — A LITTLE WHITE DOT — THAT REMAINS UNCOOKED. THIS GIVES NOODLES A FIRM FOUNDATION FOR HANDLING SAUCES AND CONTRIBUTES A FULFILLING MOUTH FEEL.

Hazelnut Chicken Breasts with Dijon Yogurt Sauce

*Roast chicken is about as American as you can get,
but adding Dijon Yogurt Sauce gives this bird an international
flavor and aroma.*

HAZELNUT CHICKEN BREASTS WITH
DIJON YOGURT SAUCE
page 31

POTATOES AU GRATIN
page 32

PORCINI AND ASPARAGUS SAUTÉ
page 33

Suggested Wine
Chardonnay

HAZELNUT CHICKEN BREASTS WITH DIJON YOGURT SAUCE

Serves 4

Matching mustard with Chardonnay may sound a bit odd, but it's actually a classic wine and food combination that I first sampled in Dijon, France, where some of the greatest White Burgundies (Chardonnays) are produced. The zesty spice of the Dijon mustard and nutty flavor of the toasted hazelnuts in this dish blend deliciously into the rich tropical fruit and butterscotch flavors of an oak-aged Chardonnay.

4   boneless, skinless chicken breast halves

1   cup toasted hazelnuts, finely chopped (see page 103)

2   tablespoons unsalted butter, softened

2   large shallots, minced

2   tablespoons plain yogurt

1   tablespoon finely chopped fresh tarragon

1   tablespoon Dijon mustard

Salt and white pepper to taste

Preheat oven to 350°F. Place chicken breasts in an oiled baking pan. Mix together the hazelnuts, butter, shallots, yogurt, tarragon, mustard, salt and pepper. Spread this mixture evenly over the tops of the chicken breasts. Bake for 20 minutes, or until golden brown. Serve in a pool of Dijon Yogurt Sauce.

DIJON YOGURT SAUCE

2   cups plain yogurt

1   tablespoon Dijon mustard

1   teaspoon sugar

1/8 teaspoon grated lemon zest

Pinch of salt

Whisk together all ingredients, mixing well. Spoon onto serving plates and top with Hazelnut Chicken Breasts.

POTATOES AU GRATIN

Serves 4 to 6

2 tablespoons butter

3 large russet potatoes, peeled and thinly sliced

2 Walla Walla sweet onions, thinly sliced

3/4 cup grated Gouda cheese

Freshly ground black pepper to taste

1 tablespoon chopped fresh oregano

1 1/2 cups milk, scalded

Preheat oven to 375°F. In an 8 1/2 -by-11-inch buttered baking dish place alternating layers of potatoes, onions and cheese, repeating layers at least three deep, ending with cheese on top. Sprinkle with black pepper and oregano.

Cover the potatoes with hot milk. Bake for one hour, or until the potatoes are tender and the top is nicely browned.

PORCINI AND ASPARAGUS SAUTÉ

Serves 4

*When fresh porcini are not available, substitute any of your favorite
wild or cultivated mushrooms.*

3 tablespoons olive oil

1 small yellow onion, thinly sliced

2 garlic cloves, minced

3 slices pancetta (Italian bacon) or
   regular bacon, diced

1/4 pound fresh porcini mushrooms, wiped
     clean with a damp cloth and sliced

1 pound asparagus, rinsed and trimmed

1/8 teaspoon ground cumin

Pinch of red pepper flakes

Juice of 1/4 lemon

Heat the olive oil in a large skillet over medium-high heat. When the oil is hot, add the onion, garlic and pancetta. Cook about 5 minutes, until the onions are tender. Add the mushrooms and asparagus and cook, stirring occasionally, just until the asparagus is tender, about 7 minutes. Season with cumin and red pepper flakes. Remove from the heat and sprinkle with lemon juice.

Wine Note

BARREL AGING

CERTAIN GRAPE VARIETALS, INCLUDING CHARDONNAY, HAVE A NATURAL AFFINITY
FOR THE RICH FLAVORS AND AROMAS IMPARTED BY OAK AGING. THE WOOD OF
TOASTED OAK BARRELS BESTOWS ITS OWN DISTINCT TONES OF SPICE, TOAST,
BUTTERSCOTCH AND VANILLA FLAVORS, WHICH BECOME MORE INTENSE AS THE
WINE AGES. THE GEOGRAPHIC ORIGIN OF THE OAK, COMMONLY FRENCH OR
AMERICAN, ALSO MAKES A SPECIFIC CONTRIBUTION TO THE FLAVOR OF THE WINE.

Italian Pounded Chicken

*This is a classic Northern Italian method for grilled chicken
that I often use for summer entertaining. The fig and prosciutto
dish is a Sarich tradition. My grandparents would serve
a platter filled with large light-skinned King figs freshly picked
from a tree that my grandfather raised from cuttings
brought from his native Croatia. It's still my favorite way
to begin a European-style meal.*

FIGS, PROSCIUTTO AND PECORINO CHEESE
page 35

ITALIAN POUNDED CHICKEN
page 36

EGGPLANT AND ZUCCHINI STRATA
page 37

Suggested Wine
Pinot Gris

FIGS, PROSCIUTTO AND PECORINO CHEESE

Serves 4 to 6

If Pecorino is not available, substitute Kasseri or Asiago cheese.

6 fresh figs, quartered

8 ounces prosciutto, thinly sliced

6 ounces Pecorino cheese

Arrange the figs and prosciutto on a chilled platter. Using a potato peeler, shave ribbons of cheese over the figs and prosciutto.

Wine Note

PINOT GRIS

THIS COUSIN OF PINOT NOIR PRODUCES A CRISP WHITE TO SLIGHTLY PINKISH WINE WITH EXOTIC FRUIT FLAVORS, FLINTY MINERALS AND CRISP, LEMONY ACIDS. CURRENTLY OREGON'S RISING STAR, PINOT GRIS IS PLANTED THROUGHOUT WESTERN EUROPE, WHERE IT IS BEST KNOWN AS THE GRAPE OF ALSACE AND AS ITALY'S PINOT GRIGIO. THIS GRAPE LENDS ITSELF TO OAK AGING AND IS ALSO DELICIOUS AGED IN STAINLESS-STEEL TANKS.

ITALIAN POUNDED CHICKEN

Serves 4

2 whole fryer chickens (approximately 3 to 4 pounds), split in half down the breast bone

1/4 cup extra-virgin olive oil

Juice of 2 lemons

1/2 cup Chardonnay or other dry white wine

1/4 cup stemmed and chopped fresh rosemary

1/4 cup finely chopped fresh Italian parsley

1/4 teaspoon dry mustard

1/2 teaspoon crushed red pepper flakes

Salt to taste

Place the chicken halves on a cutting board. Snip the skin between the joints of the wings to facilitate flattening. Using a heavy wooden mallet or the back of a heavy saucepan, pound the chicken firmly to flatten it slightly, to about 1 1/2-inch thickness. This will help the chicken lie flat on the grill.

Combine the olive oil, lemon juice, wine, rosemary, parsley, mustard, red pepper flakes and salt in a large mixing bowl. Add the chicken and marinate for 1 hour, turning occasionally. Meanwhile, heat a charcoal grill or stove-top grill. Drain the chicken and place it, skin side up, on the hot grill. Weight the chicken down using a heavy skillet or clean bricks. Cook 15 to 20 minutes, until golden. Turn the chicken, top with the weights, and cook another 15 to 20 minutes, until skin is golden and joints pull apart easily. Serve 1/2 chicken per person.

To cook Italian pounded chicken on an indoor grill: Brown the chicken (weighted down) over the grill for about 12 minutes on each side, or until golden. Transfer the chicken to a baking sheet and roast in a preheated 325°F oven for about 30 minutes, or until the chicken is cooked through.

Eggplant and Zucchini Strata

Serves 4

Meaty and rich, this vegetable strata also makes a delicious vegetarian entree. Whenever they're available, I prefer the flavor of sweet onions such as Vidalia, Texas Sweets or Walla Walla Sweets in this recipe.

1 large eggplant, sliced into 1/4-inch rounds

2 large zucchini, sliced into 1/4-inch rounds

3 large tomatoes, sliced into 1/4-inch rounds

1 large sweet or yellow onion, thinly sliced

4 balls fresh mozzarella cheese (about 3 ounces each), sliced into 1/4-inch rounds

1 cup fresh basil leaves, stemmed

1/4 cup extra-virgin olive oil

Freshly ground black pepper to taste

Salt to taste

1 1/2 cups prepared marinara sauce or diced canned tomatoes

2 tablespoons dry white wine

Preheat oven to 350°F. Oil the bottom and sides of a deep-sided 1-quart casserole or soufflé pan. Begin with a layer of eggplant, then follow with layers of zucchini, tomato, onion, mozzarella and basil. Sprinkle with 1/3 of the olive oil and season with black pepper and salt. Repeat twice, ending with a layer of basil. Pour the marinara sauce and wine over the strata. Cover and bake for 15 minutes. Uncover and continue baking 20 minutes longer, or until mixture is bubbling hot. Divide into portions and serve warm.

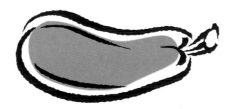

Dalmatian Coast Dinner

This aromatic "stew" is one of my favorite winter meals.
The recipe, handed down from my Croatian grandparents,
reflects the Sarich Dalmatian coast origin.

OLIVE TAPENADE
page 39

CROATIAN KRAUT, SAUSAGE AND CHICKEN STEW
page 40

APPLE STRUDEL WITH WHIDBEY'S CREAM
page 41

Suggested Wine
Sauvignon Blanc
or
Dry Riesling

OLIVE TAPENADE

Makes 1 1/2 cups
(serves 8 as an appetizer)

Serve this robust olive spread with crackers or slices of toasted French bread brushed with olive oil. The crisp, delicate fruit flavors of a chilled Sauvignon Blanc will refresh the palate between bites.

3 garlic cloves

4 anchovy fillets or 2 tablespoons anchovy paste

1 cup pitted black olives, preferably Greek or Kalamata

1/4 cup roasted red pepper

1 tablespoon chopped fresh oregano

1 tablespoon chopped fresh Italian parsley

1 tablespoon capers

1/2 teaspoon ground cumin

1 teaspoon dry mustard

1 tablespoon balsamic vinegar

Process the garlic in a blender or food processor until finely minced. Add the anchovies and purée. Add the remaining ingredients and blend until smooth. Turn into a serving dish and chill for at least 1 hour or overnight.

Chef's Tip

TO QUICK-ROAST AND PEEL PEPPERS

Broiler Method: PREHEAT BROILER. QUARTER THE PEPPERS LENGTHWISE, DISCARDING THE STEMS, SEEDS AND RIBS. PLACE THE PEPPERS, SKIN SIDE UP, ON A BAKING SHEET OR BROILER PAN. BROIL ABOUT 2 INCHES FROM THE HEAT UNTIL SKINS ARE BLISTERED AND CHARRED, 8 TO 12 MINUTES. TRANSFER PEPPERS TO A CLEAN PAPER BAG. CLOSE THE BAG AND LET STAND UNTIL PEPPERS ARE COOL ENOUGH TO HANDLE. PEEL THE PEPPERS. NOTE: IF PEPPERS ARE DIFFICULT TO PEEL, PLACE UNDER COLD RUNNING WATER WHILE PEELING. *Gas Stove Method:* LAY WHOLE PEPPERS ON TOP OF GAS BURNERS (ONE TO A BURNER). TURN THE FLAME TO HIGH AND CHAR PEPPERS, TURNING THEM WITH TONGS, UNTIL THE SKINS ARE BLACKENED, 6 TO 8 MINUTES. TRANSFER PEPPERS TO A CLEAN PAPER BAG. CLOSE THE BAG AND LET STAND UNTIL PEPPERS ARE COOL ENOUGH TO HANDLE. PEEL THE PEPPERS. CUT OFF TOPS AND DISCARD SEEDS AND RIBS.

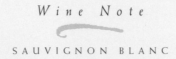
SAUVIGNON BLANC

WHILE THE AMERICAN PUBLIC REMAINS INFATUATED WITH CHARDONNAY, WINE LOVERS AROUND THE WORLD ARE DISCOVERING THE SEDUCTIVE, SOPHISTICATED WINES PRODUCED FROM SAUVIGNON BLANC — BEST KNOWN AS A PARTNER WITH SEMILLON IN WHITE BORDEAUX AND AS ONE OF THE WHITE GRAPES OF THE LOIRE VALLEY. CONSIDERED BY SOME WINE EXPERTS TO BE AMONG THE MOST DELICIOUS FOOD WINES, SAUVIGNON BLANC (ALSO KNOWN AS FUMÉ BLANC) HAS A ZESTY ACIDITY AND FRESH, CRISP FLAVORS OF MELON AND CITRUS. SOME SAUVIGNON BLANC IS AGED IN OAK, WHICH ADDS RICHNESS TO ITS FLAVOR.

CROATIAN KRAUT, SAUSAGE AND CHICKEN STEW

Serves 4

4 tablespoons olive oil

2 slices bacon, diced

4 chicken thighs

4 chicken legs

2 yellow onions, diced

3 garlic cloves, minced

1 1/2 tablespoons tomato paste

1 pound sauerkraut, rinsed twice and drained

1 tablespoon Dijon mustard

1 teaspoon chopped fresh thyme

1/8 teaspoon paprika

1 bay leaf

2 tablespoons Gewurztraminer

4 medium red potatoes, diced

Water or chicken stock to cover (see page 167)

2 kielbasa sausages, cut into 1-inch pieces

Heat the olive oil over medium-high heat in a large, heavy-bottomed saucepan. Add the bacon and cook until it becomes translucent. Add the chicken pieces and cook, turning several times, until well browned on all sides. Remove the chicken and set aside. Stir in the onion and garlic and cook until softened. Stir in the tomato paste, mixing well.

Add the sauerkraut, mustard, thyme, paprika, bay leaf, wine and potatoes. Return the chicken to the saucepan. Add just enough water or stock to cover the ingredients. Cover the pan and simmer 30 to 40 minutes, or until the potatoes start to become tender. Add the sausage. Cover and simmer 30 more minutes, stirring occasionally. Serve in large soup bowls accompanied by warm, crusty bread.

Apple Strudel with Whidbey's Cream

1/2 cup packed brown sugar

1/4 cup white sugar

1/2 cup flour

4 Granny Smith apples, peeled, cored and sliced

1/2 cup raisins soaked in Late Harvest White Riesling

1/2 cup chopped walnuts or filberts

1/8 teaspoon nutmeg

1/8 teaspoon cinnamon

Pinch of salt

1 tablespoon grated orange zest

15 sheets phyllo dough

Melted butter to coat phyllo dough

Preheat oven to 375°F. Blend sugars and flour together in a bowl. Add apples, raisins, nuts, nutmeg, cinnamon, salt and orange zest and stir to coat.

Remove the phyllo dough from the package and cover with a damp cloth to prevent it from drying out. Brush one sheet of phyllo dough with melted butter. Top with four more sheets, brushing each with melted butter. Place approximately 1/3 of the apple filling down the center. Roll up in log fashion and seal ends. Repeat with the remaining apple filling. Butter or egg-wash the top and bake for 30 minutes, or until golden brown. Cut into 2-inch slices and serve with Whidbey's Cream.

WHIDBEY'S CREAM

1 pint whipping cream

1/3 cup sour cream

Squeeze of lemon juice

2 tablespoons confectioners' sugar

2 ounces Whidbey's Loganberry Liqueur

Whip the cream until stiff peaks form. Fold the sour cream into the whipped cream. Stir in remaining ingredients and serve over or under the strudel.

One-Dish Meals and Croatian Potato Bread

One-dish meals are ideal for entertaining large groups or for fixing ahead to reheat at the end of a full day of outdoor work or play. In our house, these meals usually begin with a platter of fresh green onions, radishes and Greek olives, and they are accompanied by a warm loaf of crusty Croatian Potato Bread.

CROATIAN POTATO BREAD
page 43

HEARTY CHICKEN BEAN SOUP
page 44

SPICY CLAM PASTA
page 45

OLD COUNTRY POTATO SOUP
page 46

WINTER CHICKEN PASTA
page 47

CROATIAN POTATO BREAD

Makes 1 large round loaf

Warm from the oven, this fragrant potato bread studded with garlic and rosemary is nearly irresistible. In fact, while I'm cooking dinner, I can barely keep my hands off it. It's especially delicious washed down with a glass of chilled Sauvignon Blanc or Chardonnay.

1   tablespoon dry yeast

2   tablespoons sugar

1   cup warm water

2   medium russet potatoes, peeled and grated

2   garlic cloves, minced

1   tablespoon chopped fresh rosemary

1   tablespoon salt

3 1/2 cups unbleached all-purpose flour, approximately

Combine the yeast and sugar in a large mixing bowl. Pour the warm water over the yeast, stirring well. Let the mixture sit until the yeast has dissolved and starts to bubble, 5 to 10 minutes. Stir in the grated potato, garlic and rosemary. Let the mixture sit for 20 minutes.

Add the salt and the flour, one cup at a time, until a soft dough forms. Turn the dough onto a floured surface and knead, adding flour as necessary, until the dough is smooth and glossy (about 10 minutes). Place the dough in a large, oiled mixing bowl. Brush the top of the dough with oil; cover with plastic wrap and set in a warm place to rise until doubled in bulk, about 1 hour.

Preheat oven to 375°F. Punch the dough down and turn onto a floured surface. Form a round loaf by folding the edges of the dough in toward the center, until a stiff ball is formed. Turn the loaf over and, using the sides of your hands, tuck the sides of the loaf firmly underneath the center of the loaf. Place the loaf on an oiled baking sheet. Brush the top of the bread with oil or melted butter. Using a sharp knife, make four incisions across the top of the loaf. Cover and let rise in a warm place for about 30 minutes, or until the dough springs back immediately when pressed with a finger.

Bake for about 30 minutes, or until the bread is golden brown and emits a fragrant aroma. The loaf should sound hollow when tapped. Allow to cool at least 10 minutes before serving.

HEARTY CHICKEN BEAN SOUP

Serves 4

You'll need 2 cups cooked white navy or great northern beans for this recipe.
If you're short of time, use canned beans.

1 large stewing chicken or small whole fryer

3 carrots, chopped

1 onion, chopped

Salt and freshly ground black pepper to taste

1 tablespoon olive oil

1 onion, finely diced

2 garlic cloves, minced

3 Roma tomatoes, diced

1 head endive or escarole, cleaned and coarsely chopped

Pinch of salt

1/4 cup dry white wine

2 cups cooked white navy beans or great northern beans

Chopped fresh basil

Parmesan cheese, freshly grated

Black pepper, freshly ground, for garnish

Place the chicken in a large kettle. Cover with cold water (about 6 cups) and add the carrots and onions. Season with salt and pepper. Bring the water to a boil over high heat. Reduce the heat, cover and simmer the chicken for 30 minutes, until meat is no longer pink in the center. Transfer chicken to a platter and let cool. Strain the chicken stock through a sieve and reserve. When the chicken is cool enough to handle, skin and bone the meat. Tear the meat into large chunks and set aside.

Heat a large soup kettle over medium heat. Add the olive oil and, when hot, stir in the onions and garlic. Cook until softened, about 5 minutes. Add the tomatoes and cook 3 minutes more. Increase heat to medium-high. Add the chopped endive and cook until wilted.

Add the salt, 4 cups of the reserved chicken stock and wine. Bring the stock to a slow boil. Add the beans and reserved chicken meat and simmer for 15 minutes to heat through. Ladle the soup into large bowls. Garnish with chopped basil, grated Parmesan cheese and black pepper.

Suggested Wine
Sauvignon Blanc

SPICY CLAM PASTA

Serves 4

The inspiration for this recipe comes from my childhood. After school, I would ride my bike over to my best friend Joey Tranquilli's house. Joey's dad was always in the kitchen cooking something wonderful. The minute I entered their house, I was surrounded by the intriguing, spicy aromas of his cooking. One of my favorite dishes was Mr. Tranquilli's steamed clams spiced with garlic and herbs. Over the years, I've added a few ingredients to his basic dish to create this rich red pasta sauce studded with steamed clams.

2 tablespoons olive oil

1 red bell pepper, cored and thinly sliced

2 yellow onions, thinly sliced

4 garlic cloves, minced

12 Roma tomatoes, peeled, seeded and chopped

1/4 cup chopped fresh celery leaves

2 tablespoons chopped fresh Italian parsley

2 tablespoons chopped fresh basil

1/2 cup dry white wine

3 tablespoons olive oil

1/4 cup dry white wine

5 pounds Manila (steamer) clams, rinsed

Juice of 1 lemon

2 tablespoons chopped fresh rosemary

1/2 teaspoon crushed red pepper flakes

1 pound linguine, cooked and drained

1 cup freshly grated Parmesan cheese

Heat a large skillet over medium-high heat. Add the olive oil and, when hot, stir in the bell pepper, onions and garlic. Cook, stirring often, until softened, about 5 minutes. Add the tomatoes and simmer until soft, then add the celery leaves, parsley and basil. Stir in the 1/2 cup wine; reduce heat and simmer for 30 minutes, stirring occasionally.

Meanwhile, bring the remaining olive oil and 1/4 cup wine to a boil in a saucepan over medium-high heat. Add the clams, lemon juice, rosemary and red pepper flakes. Cover and steam until the clams open, about 4 to 8 minutes. Drain the clams, reserving 1 cup of the broth. Remove clams from their shells and roughly chop the clam meat. Add the chopped clams and the reserved clam broth to the tomato sauce; simmer for 10 minutes. Spoon the sauce over linguine and top with grated Parmesan cheese.

Suggested Wine
Sauvignon Blanc

OLD COUNTRY POTATO SOUP

Serves 6 to 8

POTATO SOUP

1 tablespoon olive oil

1 tablespoon butter

1 yellow onion, thinly sliced

2 leeks, cleaned and thinly sliced

4 garlic cloves, chopped (or as much as you can stand)

6 cups chicken stock (see page 167)

2 tablespoons dry white wine

1 bay leaf

2 whole cloves

4 russet potatoes, peeled and quartered

4 ounces wide fettuccine

Heat the olive oil and butter in a large saucepan over medium-high heat. When hot, add the onion, leeks and garlic. Cook until the onions soften, about 3 minutes. Add the chicken stock, wine, bay leaf, cloves and potatoes. Simmer until the potatoes can be pierced with a fork. Add the fettuccine and cook al dente (see page 29).

TOPPING

2 tablespoons extra-virgin olive oil

2 tablespoons chopped fresh parsley

2 tablespoons chopped fresh basil

1 cup freshly grated Parmesan cheese

2 green onions, thinly sliced

Mix all ingredients together in a small bowl. Sprinkle over the soup just before serving.

Suggested Wine
Pinot Gris

WINTER CHICKEN PASTA

Serves 4

1   3½- to 4-pound fryer or roasting chicken, divided into parts

All-purpose flour, seasoned with salt and pepper, for dredging

1   tablespoon olive oil

2   strips bacon, finely sliced

2   yellow onions, thinly sliced

4   garlic cloves, minced

1   cup chicken stock (see page 167)

1½ cups canned chopped tomatoes in purée

2   tablespoons Sauvignon Blanc or other dry white wine

2   tablespoons chopped sun-dried tomatoes

1   teaspoon capers, drained and chopped

2   tablespoons pitted and chopped Kalamata olives

Salt and freshly ground black pepper to taste

1   tablespoon minced fresh Italian parsley

1   tablespoon minced fresh basil

½ tablespoon minced fresh rosemary

4   cups cooked spaghetti or penne (see page 29)

2   cups freshly grated Parmesan cheese

Dredge the chicken pieces in the seasoned flour. Shake off the excess flour and set aside. Meanwhile, heat a large, heavy skillet over medium-high heat. Add the olive oil, and when hot, stir in the bacon. When the bacon turns golden brown, stir in the chicken pieces and brown well on both sides. Transfer the chicken and bacon to a plate.

Drain all but 1 tablespoon of the oil from the skillet. Return the skillet to the heat. When the oil is hot, add the onion and garlic. Cook until softened, about 3 minutes. Stir in the chicken stock, tomatoes, wine, sun-dried tomatoes, capers and olives. Season with salt and pepper

Simmer the sauce for 5 minutes. Add the chicken pieces to the simmering sauce. Cover and simmer for 1 hour, stirring occasionally. When the chicken is tender, remove the lid and simmer 15 more minutes. Stir in the minced parsley, basil and rosemary. Serve over spaghetti or penne and top with freshly grated Parmesan cheese.

Suggested Wine
Chardonnay

Maple-Glazed Salmon with Peach and Papaya Chutney

Fresh Spring Halibut Provençal

This is a dish I prepared with French chef Philippe Padovani at the famed Manele Bay Hotel on the Hawaiian island of Lanai.

MARINATED MUSHROOMS
page 51

CRAB–STUFFED ENDIVE
page 52

FRESH SPRING HALIBUT PROVENÇAL WITH
POACHED CUCUMBERS AND TOMATO SALAD
page 53

WILD RICE AND PORCINI PANCAKES
page 54

LEMON MOUSSE WITH STRAWBERRIES AND
WHIDBEY'S WHIPPED CREAM
page 55

Suggested Wine
Sauvignon Blanc

Marinated Mushrooms

Serves 6 to 8

1 pound button mushrooms

1/4 cup olive oil

Juice of 1 lemon

2 tablespoons Chateau Ste. Michelle Johannisberg Riesling

3 garlic cloves, mashed

1/2 teaspoon dry mustard

1/4 teaspoon ground cumin

1/4 teaspoon paprika

Pinch of red pepper flakes

1 tablespoon chopped fresh oregano

1 tablespoon chopped fresh basil

1 tablespoon chopped fresh parsley

Salt and pepper to taste

In a large nonreactive bowl, toss mushrooms with all other ingredients and marinate for 20 minutes. Sauté mushrooms in a dry skillet over high heat for 3 to 5 minutes, until just tender.

Wine Note

WINE WITH VINEGAR AND CITRUS

SOME COMMON COOKING INGREDIENTS, INCLUDING CITRUS JUICES AND VINEGAR, INCREASE ACIDITY IN FOODS AND CAUSE UNBALANCED FOOD AND WINE COMBINATIONS. SUBSTITUTING WINE FOR CITRUS JUICE OR VINEGAR IN THE PREPARATION OF DRESSINGS AND SAUCES MAKES THE DISHES MORE COMPATIBLE WHEN SERVED WITH WINE.

CRAB–STUFFED ENDIVE

Serves 8 as an appetizer

This flavorful crab filling can also be spooned into tiny lettuce leaves or hollowed-out cherry tomatoes. Shrimp and lobster make delicious variations for crab in this recipe.

16 Belgian endive leaves, approximately

1/2 pound fresh crabmeat

1/4 cup mayonnaise

1 teaspoon dry mustard

1/2 red bell pepper, finely diced

2 tablespoons grated onion

2 tablespoons grated peeled apple

Pinch of white pepper

Few drops hot red pepper sauce

Juice of 1/4 lemon

1 tablespoon minced fresh tarragon

1 garlic clove, minced

Separate the endive leaves by slicing off the stem portion and gently peeling off the leaves. Cover endive leaves with a damp cloth until ready to fill. In a mixing bowl, stir together the remaining ingredients. Spoon or pipe the mixture into prepared endive leaves. Serve chilled.

Fresh Spring Halibut Provençal with Poached Cucumbers and Tomato Salad

This dish is also delicious served at room temperature.

TOMATO SALAD

10 Roma tomatoes, peeled, seeded and thinly sliced

1/4 cup extra-virgin olive oil

2 tablespoons balsamic vinegar

1 tablespoon capers

3 anchovy fillets, finely chopped (or 2 tablespoons anchovy paste)

2 garlic cloves, minced

2 tablespoons coarsely chopped fresh basil

Salt and freshly ground black pepper to taste

Combine all ingredients in a nonreactive bowl, mixing well. Marinate at least 15 minutes to blend flavors.

POACHED CUCUMBERS

2 cups fish or chicken stock (see pages 166 and 167)

1/2 cup dry white wine

3 cucumbers, peeled, seeded and sliced into thin 4-inch-long strips

In a large saucepan, bring the stock and wine to a boil over high heat. Add the cucumbers and poach for 7 minutes. Drain and set aside.

HALIBUT

4 5-ounce halibut fillets

1/4 cup flour seasoned with 1/2 teaspoon ground black pepper and 1/2 teaspoon salt, for dusting

2 tablespoons olive oil

Lightly dust the halibut fillets with the seasoned flour. Heat the olive oil in a skillet over medium-high heat. When oil is sizzling, add the halibut. Cook 3 minutes on each side, until fish is golden and flakes apart.

To assemble, place the halibut in the center of each serving plate. Surround with poached cucumber strips and top with marinated tomatoes.

STORING WINE

MANY OF THE WINES PRODUCED THESE DAYS ARE MEANT TO BE ENJOYED YOUNG. IF YOU CONSUME THEM WITHIN TWO MONTHS OF PURCHASE, AS MANY AMERICANS DO, YOU DON'T NEED TO WORRY ABOUT STORAGE. SIMPLY PLACE YOUR BOTTLES ON THEIR SIDES IN A COOL ROOM OR CLOSET WHERE THEY'RE NOT EXPOSED TO SUNLIGHT. IF, HOWEVER, YOU FIND YOURSELF WITH A GROWING COLLECTION, YOU'LL WANT TO HOUSE THE WINES PROPERLY FOR FUTURE ENJOYMENT. YOU DON'T NEED ANYTHING FANCY — JUST A COOL, HUMID ROOM OR CLOSET (THE HUMIDITY HELPS PREVENT THE CORKS FROM DRYING OUT). RACK THE BOTTLES ON THEIR SIDES AT A TEMPERATURE OF AROUND 53 TO 59 DEGREES FAHRENHEIT. GRADUAL SEASONAL TEMPERATURE VARIATIONS ARE OKAY, BUT AVOID QUICK TEMPERATURE SWINGS AS WELL AS VIBRATION.

WILD RICE AND PORCINI PANCAKES

Serves 4

These rice cakes need to chill at least an hour before cooking and can be prepared up to one day in advance.

1   cup cooked wild rice, chilled

2   cups cooked long-grain white rice, chilled

1   large egg, lightly beaten

2   shallots, minced

2   ounces fresh porcini mushrooms, thinly sliced

2   tablespoons freshly grated Parmesan cheese

2   tablespoons fine bread crumbs

Salt to taste

1 tablespoon vegetable oil

Thoroughly combine all ingredients but the oil in a mixing bowl. Form into 6 to 8 patties about 1/2 inch thick. Cover with plastic wrap and refrigerate for 1 to 2 hours. Heat the oil in a large skillet over medium heat. When hot, add the pancakes and fry until golden brown on both sides.

LEMON MOUSSE WITH STRAWBERRIES AND WHIDBEY'S WHIPPED CREAM

Serves 4

LEMON MOUSSE

1 tablespoon unflavored gelatin

3/4 cup lemon juice

4 egg yolks

1 cup sugar

1/2 cup lime juice

1/2 cup heavy cream

1/2 cup milk

Grated zest of 4 lemons

4 egg whites

Sprinkle gelatin over 4 tablespoons of lemon juice and let soften. Beat egg yolks and 5 tablespoons of sugar until thick. In a saucepan, combine and scald the lime juice, cream, milk, remaining lemon juice, and lemon zest. Whisk together the egg yolks and cream mixture in a double boiler over medium heat until doubled in volume. Whisk in the dissolved gelatin. Combine the remaining sugar with 1/3 cup cold water in a saucepan. Cook over medium-high heat until thick bubbles form. In a separate bowl, beat egg whites until stiff. Gradually mix the sugar syrup into the egg whites, then gently fold into the egg yolk mixture. Pour into buttered or oiled molds or cake pan and refrigerate for three hours.

STRAWBERRIES

1 pint strawberries, sliced

3 ounces Whidbey's Loganberry Liqueur

Marinate strawberries for a few minutes in liqueur.

WHIDBEY'S WHIPPED CREAM

1 pint whipping cream

1/4 – 1/2 cup crème fraîche (or substitute sour cream)

2 ounces Whidbey's Loganberry Liqueur

1/8 teaspoon grated lemon zest

3 tablespoons confectioners' sugar

Whip cream until almost stiff. Mix in crème fraîche, liqueur, zest and sugar.

To serve, unmold the mousse, cover with strawberries and top with whipped cream.

Maple-Glazed Salmon with Peach and Papaya Chutney

This is a quick, elegant dish that I often serve at the winery in the spring, when the first Alaskan Copper River king salmon becomes available. These wild salmon are highly prized for their rich oil content, which translates into superb flavor.

SPINACH AND SCALLOP SALAD

page 57

MAPLE-GLAZED SALMON WITH
PEACH AND PAPAYA CHUTNEY

page 58

QUICK VEGETABLE STIR-FRY

page 59

STEAMED JASMINE RICE

page 60

QUICK CHERRY TART

page 61

Suggested Wines
Chardonnay
Late Harvest White Riesling

SPINACH AND SCALLOP SALAD

Serves 4

1/2 cup Johannisberg Riesling

Juice of 1/2 lemon

Pinch of salt

Pinch of white pepper

1 garlic clove, mashed

1/4 cup olive oil

1 pound Northwest scallops

2/3 cup walnut oil

1/4 cup raspberry vinegar

1 tablespoon Dijon mustard

1 tablespoon chopped shallots

1 teaspoon chopped fresh tarragon

1/4 cup heavy cream

Salt and white pepper to taste

1 bunch fresh spinach, washed and dried

1 red onion, thinly sliced

In a nonreactive bowl, combine Riesling, lemon juice, salt, white pepper, garlic and olive oil. Mix well. Add scallops and marinate at least one hour. Heat a charcoal grill or stove-top grill until hot. Skewer the scallops and grill until just golden. Cool and set aside.

Blend walnut oil, vinegar, mustard, shallots, tarragon, cream, salt and pepper together. Toss the scallops, spinach and red onion with the dressing and arrange on serving plates.

MAPLE–GLAZED SALMON WITH PEACH AND PAPAYA CHUTNEY

Serves 4

1 1½- to 2-pound salmon fillet

1 cup apple juice

1 cup real maple syrup

Juice of 1 lemon

Salt to taste

Preheat oven to 425°F. Remove the pin bones from the salmon fillet using tweezers or small needle-nose pliers. Place the salmon in an oiled nonreactive baking pan. In a nonreactive bowl, mix together the apple juice, maple syrup, lemon juice and salt. Brush the salmon generously with this mixture, reserving some for basting. Bake for about 15 to 20 minutes, basting and checking frequently for doneness. The salmon is cooked as soon as the last bit of meat in the center loses its bright color. Divide the salmon into serving portions and serve warm with Peach and Papaya Chutney.

PEACH AND PAPAYA CHUTNEY

1 ripe papaya, diced

2 ripe peaches, peeled and diced

Juice of ½ lemon

½ red onion, diced

½ teaspoon fresh ginger, thinly sliced

1 shallot, finely diced

1 tablespoon peanut oil

1 teaspoon rice wine vinegar

¼ teaspoon Asian sesame oil

1 tablespoon chopped fresh cilantro

In a nonreactive bowl, mix together the papaya, peaches and lemon juice. Add the red onion, ginger, shallot, peanut oil, vinegar, sesame oil and cilantro. Mix thoroughly. Serve at room temperature with Maple-Glazed Salmon.

QUICK VEGETABLE STIR–FRY

S e r v e s 4

*If desired, serve these crisp vegetables over steamed jasmine rice or saifun
(mung bean or glass) noodles.*

2 tablespoons peanut oil

1 red bell pepper, julienned

1 yellow bell pepper, julienned

1 yellow onion, julienned

1 cup broccoli florets

1/3 cup sliced fresh shiitake mushrooms

1 garlic clove, minced

5 thin slices fresh ginger

1/3 cup chicken stock (see page 167)

2 teaspoons Vietnamese fish sauce

2 teaspoons soy sauce

Heat a wok or large heavy-bottomed skillet over high heat. When the pan is hot, add the peanut oil. When the oil begins to smoke, stir in the peppers and onion, stirring constantly. Cook 2 minutes. Add the broccoli, mushrooms, garlic and ginger and cook, stirring constantly, for 2 more minutes. Stir in the chicken stock, fish sauce and soy sauce. Simmer for about 1 more minute. Vegetables should be tender but still maintain a crispness when you bite into them.

CHOOSING RICE

THERE IS A WIDE VARIETY OF RICE AVAILABLE IN MOST GROCERY STORES. I USUALLY SERVE A RICE THAT REFLECTS THE REGIONAL CUISINE OF THE MAIN COURSE, SUCH AS ITALIAN ARBORIO FOR RISOTTO OR JASMINE WITH ASIAN CUISINE.

STEAMED JASMINE RICE

Serves 4

2 cups water

1 cup Jasmine rice

1 tablespoon sweet butter

In a heavy-bottomed saucepan with a tight-fitting lid, bring water to a slow boil. Stir in rice. Reduce heat to medium-low, cover and cook for 20 minutes. Spoon cooked rice into serving bowl, top with butter and serve immediately.

QUICK CHERRY TART

Serves 8
(Makes one 9-inch tart)

2 cups finely ground vanilla wafers

1/4 cup unsalted butter, melted

1/2 cup cream cheese, softened

1 cup sour cream

1 teaspoon sugar

1/2 teaspoon grated lemon zest

1/2 teaspoon vanilla

2 cups pitted Bing cherries

Fresh mint leaves, for garnish

Combine the vanilla wafer crumbs and melted butter in a mixing bowl. Turn into a 9-inch pie pan. Using a spoon, press the crumbs evenly around the bottom and edges of the pie pan. Chill the crust in the refrigerator. Meanwhile, whip the cream cheese until smooth. Fold in the sour cream, sugar, lemon zest and vanilla, mixing well. Fold in the cherries. Pour the mixture into the prepared pie crust. Chill for at least 2 hours, or overnight. Divide into serving portions and garnish with mint leaves.

Suggested Wine
Late Harvest White Riesling

Veal Loin with Sweet Pepper Purée

Sweet pepper purée adds a rich silkiness to veal loin.
The smoky quality of the oak-aged Chardonnay in the
marinade complements both the flavor and aroma of this dish
as well as the fresh greens and garlic sauté.

VEAL LOIN WITH SWEET PEPPER PURÉE
page 63

FRESH GREENS AND GARLIC SAUTÉ
page 64

PEACH PIE
page 65

Suggested Wines
Chardonnay
Late Harvest White Riesling

VEAL LOIN WITH SWEET PEPPER PURÉE

Serves 6

1   2-pound boneless veal loin, approximately

1/4 cup Chardonnay or other dry white wine

2   tablespoons olive oil

2   garlic cloves, minced

2   tablespoons chopped fresh parsley

1   tablespoon chopped fresh thyme

1   tablespoon chopped fresh rosemary

2   tablespoons Dijon mustard

Juice of 1/2 lemon

Salt and white pepper to taste

Trim the veal loin. Combine the remaining ingredients in a nonreactive mixing bowl. Coat the veal loin evenly with the marinade. Cover with plastic wrap and chill for one hour.

Preheat oven to 375°F. Preheat an indoor grill or heat a heavy-bottomed saucepan over high heat. Drain the veal, discarding the marinade. Sear the veal evenly on the grill or stove top until golden. Transfer the veal to a baking pan. Bake, uncovered, for about 20 minutes, or until the veal reaches an internal temperature of 160°F. Transfer to a platter and keep warm. Reserve pan juices for the Sweet Pepper Purée.

SWEET PEPPER PURÉE

1/4 cup olive oil

2   red bell peppers, sliced

2   yellow bell peppers, sliced

2   yellow onions, sliced

2   garlic cloves, minced

1/2 teaspoon Hungarian paprika

1/2 teaspoon balsamic vinegar

Reserved pan juices from veal

Salt to taste

Heat the olive oil over medium-high heat in a skillet. When hot, add the peppers, onions and garlic. Cook until the vegetables have softened, about 5 minutes. Stir in the paprika, vinegar, pan juices and salt. Transfer the mixture to a blender or food processor and purée until smooth.

To serve, cut the veal in 1/4-inch slices. Fan three or four slices over each serving plate and drizzle the Sweet Pepper Purée over the veal.

FRESH GREENS AND GARLIC SAUTÉ

Serves 4

1 tablespoon olive oil

2 garlic cloves, whole

2 bunches spinach, washed and stemmed

1 teaspoon balsamic vinegar

Heat a large sauté pan over medium-high heat. Add olive oil and when sizzling, add the garlic cloves and sauté until golden. Place spinach in pan and sauté until just wilted. Stir in balsamic vinegar.

PEACH PIE

4 cups peeled and sliced ripe peaches

1 tablespoon lemon juice

1/2 teaspoon grated orange zest

1/4 teaspoon cinnamon

1/8 teaspoon ground cloves

1/2 cup all-purpose flour

1/2 cup firmly packed brown sugar

1/2 cup sugar

Pinch of salt

Pastry for 9-inch double-crust pie

2 tablespoons unsalted butter

Preheat oven to 350°F. In a large mixing bowl, combine the sliced peaches with the lemon juice, orange zest, cinnamon, cloves, flour, brown sugar, sugar and salt, mixing well. Divide the pastry into two pieces and roll out. Line a 9-inch pie pan with 1/2 of the dough. Pour the peach mixture into the lined pie pan and dot with the butter. Make four small incisions on the top crust for vents. Lay the dough over the pie. Trim the edges of the pastry and crimp together. Bake the pie for about 40 minutes, or until the pastry is golden and juice bubbles through the top crust. Serve warm or at room temperature.

Suggested Wine
Late Harvest White Riesling

Wine Note

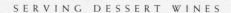

SERVING DESSERT WINES

SERVE SWEET WINES SLIGHTLY CHILLED AS APERITIFS OR AFTER–DINNER DRINKS, OR PAIRED WITH DESSERTS OF COMPLEMENTARY SWEETNESS AND COMPLEXITY. THE MORE FLAVORFUL, SWEET AND COMPLEX A WINE IS, THE BETTER IT WILL TASTE WITH RICH, ELABORATE DESSERTS. HOWEVER, CHOCOLATE IS ONE OF THE FEW FLAVORS THAT DOES NOT PAIR WELL WITH LATE HARVEST WINES. THE TANNINS IN THE CHOCOLATE COUNTERACT THE HONEYED SWEETNESS OF THE WINE, PRODUCING CONFLICTING FLAVORS.

Chinese Barbecued Pork Roast

Chinese Barbecued Pork Celebration

My own cooking style is best described as Pacific Northwest cuisine, but I love Chinese food. Barbecued pork roast is a great dish to cook ahead for entertaining. It does require some time to prepare but it's worth the effort.

DUNGENESS CRAB SPRING ROLLS

page 69

CHINESE BARBECUED PORK ROAST

page 70

GINGER FRIED RICE

page 71

ASPARAGUS WITH BLACK BEAN SAUCE

page 72

LYCHEE NUTS AND TANGERINES IN WHITE RIESLING

page 73

Suggested Wine
Dry Riesling
or
Semillon

Dungeness Crab Spring Rolls with Ginger–Sesame Dipping Sauce

Serves 4 to 6

These crisp rolls are equally delicious made with shrimp.

8   ounces ground pork

1   tablespoon peanut oil

1/4 teaspoon Asian sesame oil

1   tablespoon grated fresh ginger

2   garlic cloves, minced

1   tablespoon dry fermented black beans

1   tablespoon red pepper sauce

8   ounces Dungeness crab meat or raw chopped shrimp meat

3   green onions, finely chopped

1/4 cup chopped fresh cilantro

6   sheets phyllo dough

1/4 cup olive oil

1   egg white

Heat a skillet over medium-high heat. Add the ground pork, peanut oil and sesame oil. Cook, stirring often, until the pork is cooked through. Stir in the ginger, garlic, fermented black beans and red pepper sauce. Remove the pan from the heat. Stir in the crab, green onions and cilantro. Set the mixture aside to cool.

Meanwhile, preheat oven to 350°F Remove the phyllo dough from the package and cover with a damp cloth to prevent it from drying out. Whisk together the olive oil and egg white.

To make the rolls, separate one sheet of phyllo dough. Brush it lightly with the olive oil mixture. Top with a second sheet of phyllo. Brush the second layer with the olive oil mixture. Top with another layer of phyllo.

With the longer edge of the phyllo dough facing you, spread half of the crab mixture across the bottom edge of the dough, leaving a 1-inch border on the bottom and sides. Roll the crab mixture tightly in the phyllo dough to create a long, thin roll about 1 1/2 inches in diameter. Tuck the ends of the dough under the roll. Set the roll on an ungreased baking sheet and brush with the olive oil mixture. Repeat to form another roll. Bake the rolls for 12 to 15 minutes, or until crisp and golden.

GINGER–SESAME DIPPING SAUCE

1/3 cup soy sauce

2   tablespoons rice wine vinegar

1/8 teaspoon Asian sesame oil

2   garlic cloves, minced

1/4 teaspoon grated fresh ginger

1   tablespoon chopped fresh cilantro

Whisk together ingredients for the sauce. Slice each roll diagonally into six portions and set on a serving plate. Serve with Ginger–Sesame Dipping Sauce.

Chef's Tip

COOKING WITH WINE

LIKE HERBS, EVERY VARIETAL HAS ITS OWN CHARACTERISTIC FLAVOR. REDUCING WINES IN COOKING (CONDENSING THEM OVER HEAT) INTENSIFIES THOSE FLAVORS AND HEIGHTENS THE IMPRESSION OF THE WINE'S CHARACTERISTICS ON THE PALATE. WHEN YOU COOK WITH THE SAME WINE YOU ARE POURING WITH DINNER, YOU CREATE A DELICIOUS BRIDGE BETWEEN THE FLAVORS OF THE WINE AND FOOD.

CHINESE BARBECUED PORK ROAST

Serves 4 to 6

This is a great dish to cook ahead for entertaining or picnics; it tastes just as good served at room temperature as it does warm.

1 1/2 cups chicken stock (see page 167)

1/2 cup ketchup

1/2 cup soy sauce

2 tablespoons Dry Riesling

2 tablespoons grated fresh ginger

2 tablespoons chopped fresh cilantro

5 fennel seeds, crushed

2 tablespoons honey

1 tablespoon sugar

2 tablespoons peanut oil

1/4 teaspoon Asian sesame oil

1/4 teaspoon hot chili oil

1 tablespoon rice wine vinegar

1 3-pound pork loin roast

In a medium saucepan, whisk together all ingredients but the pork. Bring the mixture to a boil over medium-high heat; reduce heat and simmer for 30 minutes.

Meanwhile, preheat oven to 325°F. Place the pork loin in an ovenproof baking dish and baste liberally with the sauce. Roast approximately 1 1/2 hours, basting frequently, until the internal temperature reaches 175°F. Slice thinly and serve warm.

GINGER FRIED RICE

Serves 4 to 6

3 slices bacon, diced

2 tablespoons peanut oil

1 large yellow onion, diced

1/2 cup diced celery

1 red bell pepper, diced

1 tablespoon grated fresh ginger

1 garlic clove, minced

4 cups cooked white rice, chilled

1 tablespoon chopped fresh cilantro

1 can water chestnuts, drained and sliced

4 large eggs

1/4 cup cold water

2 tablespoons soy sauce

Heat a wok or large skillet over medium heat. Add the bacon and cook until crisp. Drain the bacon on paper towels and reserve. Discard the bacon grease. Reheat the wok over medium-high heat. When hot, add the peanut oil and heat until the oil just begins to smoke. Stir in the onion, celery, bell pepper, ginger and garlic. Cook until just tender, about 4 minutes. Add the rice and fry until the rice starts to brown, stirring gently. Add the cilantro, water chestnuts and reserved bacon and heat through.

In a mixing bowl, whisk together the eggs, water and soy sauce. Pour over the rice mixture and let sit for 5 seconds. Gently mix the eggs into the rice, stirring gently until the eggs are cooked through.

ASPARAGUS WITH BLACK BEAN SAUCE

Serves 4

1 tablespoon peanut oil

1/8 teaspoon Asian sesame oil

1 yellow onion, thinly sliced

1/4 pound shiitake mushrooms, thinly sliced

2 bunches fresh asparagus, trimmed and cleaned

1 tablespoon thinly sliced fresh ginger

2 garlic cloves, thinly sliced

2 tablespoons dry fermented black beans

1/4 cup chicken stock (see page 167)

2 tablespoons soy sauce

Heat a wok or sauté pan over high heat. Add the peanut oil and sesame oil and, when hot, stir in the onions, shiitake mushrooms and asparagus. Sauté for 3 minutes, stirring often. Add the ginger, garlic and black beans and cook for another 2 minutes. Add the chicken stock and soy sauce. Continue cooking until the asparagus is just tender.

LYCHEE NUTS AND TANGERINES IN WHITE RIESLING

Serves 4

2 cups fresh or canned lychee nuts

2 fresh tangerines, peeled and segmented

1/4 cup White Riesling

Mix all the ingredients together in a nonreactive bowl. Chill for 1 hour before serving.

Chef's Tip

LOCATING LYCHEE NUTS

LYCHEE NUTS ARE NATIVE TO CHINA AND CAN BE PURCHASED FRESH AT MOST CHINESE MARKETS DURING THEIR PEAK MONTHS OF JUNE AND JULY. THE DELICATELY FLAVORED, OPAQUE FRUIT IS ENCASED IN A BRITTLE REDDISH–BROWN SHELL. TO USE FRESH LYCHEES, SIMPLY PEEL OFF THE SHELL. IF FRESH LYCHEES AREN'T AVAILABLE, CANNED LYCHEE NUTS MAKE A FINE SUBSTITUTE.

Apple and Prune Stuffed Pork Tenderloin

I served this to the Swedish Culinary Olympic Team on their visit to Chateau Ste. Michelle. The combination of fruit and meat is traditional in Scandinavian cooking.

SMOKED CHICKEN AND SPINACH SALAD
page 75

APPLE AND PRUNE STUFFED PORK TENDERLOIN
page 76

BAKED HERBED POTATOES
page 77

BROCCOLI WITH PANCETTA
page 78

WALNUT POVITICA
page 79

Suggested Wines
Sauvignon Blanc
or
Johannisberg Riesling
Late Harvest White Riesling

SMOKED CHICKEN AND SPINACH SALAD

Serves 4 to 6

1/2 cup fresh tarragon leaves

1/4 cup fresh Italian parsley

2 garlic cloves

2 tablespoons olive oil

1 – 2 tablespoons white wine vinegar

1 tablespoon Dijon mustard

1 tablespoon capers

2 tablespoons mayonnaise

1/8 teaspoon paprika

Pinch of sugar

Pinch of salt

1 head romaine lettuce

3 cups mixed field greens

1/2 cup julienned smoked chicken breast

2 tomatoes, cut into wedges

12 asparagus spears, blanched

1 red onion, thinly sliced

In a blender, purée the tarragon, parsley, garlic and olive oil. Add the vinegar, mustard, capers, mayonnaise, paprika, sugar and salt and mix thoroughly.

Construct the salad by placing romaine leaves (whole) in a star fashion on a chilled plate. Toss the field greens with a little of the dressing and place in the middle of the leaves. Place the chicken meat on top of greens. Arrange tomato and asparagus around the salad. Place red onion slices on top of salad. Drizzle more dressing over the entire salad.

Wine Note

BALANCE

ACID, TANNIN, FRUIT, ALCOHOL AND SUGAR ARE THE MAJOR COMPONENTS OF WINE. GREAT WINES COMBINE THESE ELEMENTS IN SUCH PERFECT PROPORTION THAT NONE DOMINATE, NONE RECEDE. SUCH WINE IS PERFECTION ON THE PALATE — SEAMLESS AND HARMONIOUS.

Apple and Prune Stuffed Pork Tenderloin

Serves 4 to 6

12 pitted prunes

2 apples, peeled, cored and thinly sliced

1/4 cup Sauvignon Blanc or other dry
    white wine

1 1 1/2- to 2-pound pork tenderloin

Heavy cotton kitchen twine

1/2 teaspoon dried thyme

1/2 teaspoon dry mustard

1 1/2 teaspoons salt

1/2 teaspoon freshly ground black pepper

2 tablespoons butter or vegetable oil

2 cups chicken stock or water (see
    page 167)

Place the prunes and sliced apples in a
nonreactive mixing bowl. Cover with the
Sauvignon Blanc. Meanwhile, using the
handle of a wooden spoon, bore a 1 1/2-
inch hole lengthwise through the center
of the pork. Drain the fruit and fill the
center of the tenderloin alternately with
the prunes and apple slices. Secure the
tenderloin with strong cotton string, to
retain its shape while baking.

Combine the thyme, mustard, salt and
pepper in a bowl. Rub the pork with this
mixture, distributing it evenly.

Meanwhile, heat a skillet over medium-
high heat. Add the butter. When sizzling, add the pork and brown the meat
evenly on all sides. Pour the chicken
stock over the pork. Cover the pot and
simmer until the meat is tender, about
1 hour.

To serve, cut the pork into 1/2-inch slices.
Serve with pan juices on the side.

BAKED HERBED POTATOES

Serves 4

1 pound new red potatoes, scrubbed

2 tablespoons olive oil

1 tablespoon minced fresh oregano

1 onion, coarsely diced

Salt and freshly ground black pepper
   to taste

Preheat oven to 350°F. Combine all of
the ingredients in a large baking pan,
mixing well. Bake for 1 hour, or until
golden, stirring occasionally.

Chef's Tip

SUBSTITUTING HERBS

MANY OF MY RECIPES CALL FOR FRESH HERBS AND IT'S WORTH THE EFFORT TO
FIND THEM. IF YOU MUST SUBSTITUTE DRIED HERBS, USE HALF THE QUANTITY
SUGGESTED IN THE RECIPE.

BROCCOLI WITH PANCETTA

Serves 4 to 6

1 pound broccoli, cleaned, stems trimmed, and quartered

1 tablespoon olive oil

4 tablespoons diced pancetta (Italian bacon) or 2 slices bacon, diced

1 garlic clove, minced

Pinch of salt

Blanch the broccoli in boiling water just until it can be pierced with a fork. Rinse with cold water and drain. Meanwhile, heat the olive oil in a skillet over medium heat. Add the pancetta and garlic. Cook until pancetta is golden on the edges. (If using bacon, strain off bacon grease.) Add the broccoli and cook quickly, stirring occasionally, for 3 minutes, or until heated through. Salt to taste.

WALNUT POVITICA

Makes 2 loaves (approximately 10 slices each)

This is a traditional Mediterranean dessert bread that my mom makes every holiday season. Her face glows with pride when she presents the bread to us, knowing that we've been looking forward to it all year.

2 cups milk

1/2 cup (1 stick) unsalted butter, softened

1/2 cup sugar

1 package dry yeast

2 tablespoons warm tap water

6 cups all-purpose flour, approximately

4 large egg yolks, lightly beaten

1 tablespoon salt

1 1/2 pounds walnuts, ground

1 1/2 cups half-and-half

1 cup packed brown sugar

1/2 cup white sugar

1/2 cup honey

1 tablespoon cinnamon

4 tablespoons butter

Splash of Late Harvest White Riesling

2 eggs

Scald the milk in a saucepan over medium-high heat. Remove from the heat. Add the butter and sugar, stirring until butter has melted. Set aside.

Place the yeast in a large mixing bowl. Pour warm water over the yeast, and let sit until yeast starts to bubble. Stir in the slightly warm milk mixture. Stir in 3 cups flour, mixing well. Add the beaten egg yolks and salt, mixing well. Add the remaining flour 1 cup at a time, mixing well after each addition, until a soft dough forms. Add flour if necessary.

Turn the dough onto a floured surface and knead for 10 minutes, incorporating more flour as necessary, until the dough no longer sticks to the surface and is smooth and pliable. Turn the dough into a clean, oiled bowl; cover with plastic wrap and let rise in a warm place until doubled, about 1 hour.

Meanwhile make the filling. Mix together walnuts, half-and-half, brown sugar, white sugar, honey, cinnamon, butter and wine in a saucepan and bring to a boil, stirring constantly. Remove from heat and cool slightly. Add the eggs and beat well.

Punch the dough down; cover and let rise again until doubled in bulk. Turn the dough onto a clean, floured surface and roll out into a rectangle, approximately 1/8 to 1/4 inch thick. Trim the edges and spread the dough evenly with the walnut filling. Roll the dough around the filling, as you would a jelly roll. Slice the roll into two equal lengths. Pinch the ends together to seal. Place the rolls in a well-buttered baking pan, leaving at least 3 inches between them. Cover with a cloth and let rise about 15 minutes.

Meanwhile, preheat oven to 300°F. Bake the rolls for about 1 hour, or until golden brown. Brush with butter and cool to room temperature on the baking sheets. To serve, cut into 1/2-inch-thick slices.

Red Wine Foods

Red wine is a part of my earliest memories. My grandfather made it, and I used to help crush the California Zinfandel grapes purchased from Seattle fruit merchant Tony Picardo for his best wines.

Red wines vary in character from light and fruit-flavored to rich and full-flavored. Both red and white wines start out as nearly colorless grape juice: color develops in reds when the grape juice sits in contact with the dark-colored skins. Along with their gift of color, the skins contribute distinct textures and flavors to red wine.

Pinot Noir is one of the lighter red wines produced in the Pacific Northwest. Like white wine, it has a refreshing quality, but unlike white wine, it has tannin and berry flavors. It is the perfect complement to braised meats and roast chicken.

Merlot, Cabernet Sauvignon, Cabernet Franc, Syrah and Meritage are full-flavored red wines with pronounced spiced aromas. These robust wines are well suited to lamb and beef. With its rich fruit flavor, Merlot goes well with anything from a good old-fashioned hamburger to a lamb shank feast. For dessert, pair a barrel-aged Cabernet Sauvignon with bittersweet chocolate. Believe me, that's worth celebrating.

Red Wine Menus

WEEKDAYS

SAVORY SHANKS
Suggested Wine
Merlot
page 86

DOWN HOME BARBECUE
Suggested Wine
Cabernet Sauvignon
page 90

ASIAN HONEY–SPICED RIBS
Suggested Wine
Merlot
page 96

WILD MUSHROOM PASTA
Suggested Wine
Cabernet Sauvignon
page 100

CABERNET GRILLED SIRLOIN
Suggested Wine
Cabernet Sauvignon
page 104

ONE–DISH WEEKDAY MEALS
page 110

WEEKENDS

LAMB WITH GINGER–MERLOT SAUCE
Suggested Wine
Merlot
page 118

SPIEDINI MISTI
Suggested Wine
Cabernet Franc
page 124

GAME HENS IN RED WINE SAUCE
Suggested Wine
Cabernet Franc
p a g e   1 2 8

TUSCAN CHICKEN WITH FRESH ROSEMARY
Suggested Wine
Red Meritage
p a g e   1 3 4

BRAISED RABBIT WITH CHERRIES
Suggested Wine
Red Meritage
p a g e   1 4 0

AUTUMN BRAISED SHORT RIBS
Suggested Wine
Cabernet Sauvignon
p a g e   1 4 4

HALIBUT WITH ROASTED SHALLOT–PINOT SAUCE
Suggested Wine
Pinot Noir
p a g e   1 4 8

CELEBRATIONS

MEDITERRANEAN COUSCOUS
Suggested Wine
Syrah
p a g e   1 5 6

ASIAN DUCK IN PLUM SAUCE
Suggested Wine
Merlot
p a g e   1 6 0

Smoked Chicken Crostini & Grilled Feta-Stuffed Grape Leaves

Savory Shanks

Autumn sneaks up slowly in the Pacific Northwest.
Nights turn gradually cooler as the sun dips lower in the sky,
turning trees and grapevines brilliant shades of red, orange and
gold. This is the time of year when I start thinking about
cooking long-braised dishes, like lamb shanks, that fill the
house with wonderful smells.

BRAISED LAMB SHANKS
page 87

POLENTA WITH ROASTED GARLIC AND PARMESAN
page 88

DILLED PEAS IN BUTTER SAUCE
page 89

Suggested Wine
Merlot

BRAISED LAMB SHANKS

Serves 4

4 lamb shanks (4 – 6 ounces each)

1/4 cup flour, seasoned with 1 teaspoon salt and 1/2 teaspoon black pepper, for dredging

2 tablespoons olive oil

1 large yellow onion, thinly sliced

3 garlic cloves, minced

1 cup diced Roma tomatoes

1 tablespoon tomato paste

1 cup Merlot

1 tablespoon chopped fresh rosemary

1 bay leaf

1 tablespoon chopped fresh Italian parsley

1/2 tablespoon dry mustard

1 clove

Salt and freshly ground black pepper to taste

Preheat oven to 350°F. Dredge the lamb shanks in the seasoned flour. Shake off excess flour and set aside. Heat a heavy ovenproof skillet over medium-high heat. Add the olive oil and, when sizzling, add the lamb shanks. Cook, turning occasionally, until golden brown on all sides. Remove the shanks and set aside. Add the onion and garlic. Cook, stirring often, until softened, about 5 minutes. Add the tomatoes, tomato paste, wine, rosemary, bay leaf, parsley, mustard, clove, salt and pepper. When the mixture comes to a simmer, add the lamb shanks.

Transfer the skillet to the preheated oven and bake for about 1 hour, basting occasionally with the sauce, or until the lamb is very tender. Top the lamb shanks with a generous amount of sauce before serving.

Wine Note

MERLOT

WITH ITS VELVETY TEXTURE AND RICH, OPULENT FRUIT, EASY-DRINKING MERLOT FROM WASHINGTON'S COLUMBIA VALLEY HAS BECOME A NATIONWIDE PHENOMENON. THIS SUPERSTAR OF THE PACIFIC NORTHWEST IS ALSO THE MOST-FREQUENTLY PLANTED GRAPE VARIETY IN BORDEAUX, WHERE IT IS OFTEN BLENDED WITH CABERNET SAUVIGNON AND CABERNET FRANC. LUSCIOUS FRUIT FLAVORS OF BLACK CHERRY AND BLACKBERRY UNFOLD INTO NOTES OF TOAST, VANILLA AND CINNAMON SPICE.

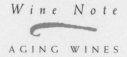
POLENTA WITH ROASTED GARLIC AND PARMESAN

Serves 4 to 6

*The secret to making creamy polenta, which I learned at my grandmother's
side, is to add the polenta very gradually, stirring constantly between
additions. A sturdy, high-sided saucepan works best.* ·

2½ cups chicken stock (see page 167)

1 cup polenta (coarse-grained cornmeal)

1 garlic bulb, roasted (see page 107)

1 tablespoon butter

2 tablespoons whipping cream

½ cup grated Parmesan cheese

Salt to taste

Bring the chicken stock to a slow simmer over medium heat in a deep, heavy-bottomed saucepan. Gradually add the polenta, ¼ cup at a time, and cook, stirring constantly, for about 15 to 20 minutes, or until the polenta becomes creamy. If necessary, add more liquid. When the polenta is cooked, stir in the garlic, butter, cream and Parmesan cheese. Season with salt. Serve warm.

DILLED PEAS IN BUTTER SAUCE

Serves 6

I use a microwave to cook these peas. You can also cook them in boiling water, just until tender. Drain the peas before adding the butter and seasonings.

3 cups fresh or frozen peas

¼ cup water

1 tablespoon unsalted butter

1 teaspoon chopped fresh dill

Salt and freshly ground black pepper to taste

Place the peas in a microwave-safe bowl. Pour in the water and dot with butter. Sprinkle with fresh dill. Cover the bowl with plastic wrap. Cook in a microwave oven on high heat for 3 minutes. Season with salt and pepper. Serve hot.

Down Home Barbecue

Barbecued burgers with fresh herbs, fresh salsa and a great Cabernet Sauvignon is simply my favorite summertime picnic menu. My kids love it, too. It's quick, simple and very full-flavored.

APPLE AND CABBAGE SLAW

page 91

CHOPPED SIRLOIN AND FRESH HERB BURGERS

page 92

SPICY PICKLED GREEN TOMATOES

page 93

TOMATO–PEACH SALSA

page 94

FRESH RASPBERRY PURÉE WITH
FRENCH VANILLA ICE CREAM

page 95

Suggested Wine
Cabernet Sauvignon

APPLE AND CABBAGE SLAW

2 cups green cabbage, thinly grated or sliced

2 cups red cabbage, thinly grated or sliced

1 yellow onion, grated

1 tart apple, grated

2 tablespoons mayonnaise

1 tablespoon olive oil

2 tablespoons white wine vinegar

1/8 teaspoon caraway seeds, chopped

Salt and freshly ground black pepper to taste

Splash of Tabasco sauce (optional)

Mix all ingredients together in a non-reactive bowl. Refrigerate for 1 hour before serving.

CABERNET SAUVIGNON

CABERNET SAUVIGNON IS CONSIDERED BY MANY TO BE ONE OF THE WORLD'S NOBLEST GRAPES. BEST KNOWN AS THE FOUNDATION OF THE AGE–WORTHY RED WINES OF THE MÉDOC DISTRICT OF BORDEAUX, CABERNET SAUVIGNON WAS FIRST PLANTED IN WASHINGTON STATE IN THE 1960S. WARM DAYS AND COOL NIGHTS, DEEP, SANDY LOAM SOILS AND EXTRA–LONG DAYLIGHT HOURS ALL CONTRIBUTE TO THE PRODUCTION OF BEAUTIFULLY BALANCED, COMPLEX WINES HERE. RICH, OPULENT FLAVORS OF FRUIT AND SPICE ARE FRAMED BY FIRM TANNINS AND ELEGANT STRUCTURE, MAKING THESE WINES DELICIOUS WHEN YOUNG AND GIVING THEM THE POTENTIAL TO AGE GRACEFULLY FOR WELL OVER A DECADE.

CHOPPED SIRLOIN AND FRESH HERB BURGERS

M a k e s   8   b u r g e r s

1 1/2 pounds lean chopped sirloin

1   small yellow onion, grated

1   garlic clove, minced

2   tablespoons freshly grated Parmesan cheese

1   tablespoon chopped fresh Italian parsley

1/2 tablespoon chopped fresh oregano

1   teaspoon Worcestershire sauce

1/2 teaspoon freshly ground black pepper

1   teaspoon salt

Preheat a grill or broiler to medium-high. Combine all ingredients in a mixing bowl and knead until thoroughly blended. Divide the mixture into eight portions and flatten into 1/3-inch patties. Sear the meat by cooking 2 minutes on each side over the hottest part of the grill. Then move the patties to lower heat for another 2 minutes per side, or to an internal temperature of 165°F.

SPICY PICKLED GREEN TOMATOES

Makes 2 quarts

Here's a delicious way to use up green tomatoes from your garden.

2 pounds green tomatoes, quartered

2 cups cider vinegar

1 cup water

1/2 cup Dry Riesling

1/3 cup sugar

1 tablespoon pickling spice

1 tablespoon whole black peppercorns

1 bay leaf

4 garlic cloves, whole

2 medium yellow onions, sliced thick

2 small cayenne peppers, whole

2 sprigs fresh dill

2 sterilized quart jars with lids

Combine the tomatoes, vinegar, water, wine, sugar, pickling spice, peppercorns, bay leaf and 2 garlic cloves in a saucepan. Bring to a boil over high heat. Reduce heat and simmer for 10 minutes. Remove from the heat and set aside to cool slightly.

Pack the tomatoes and onions in the jars. Add 1 cayenne pepper, 1 sprig of dill and 1 garlic clove to each jar. Fill the jars to 1/2 inch from the top with the brine and seal with sterilized lids. Cover with water, bring to a boil, and process in a water bath for 15 minutes, following manufacturer's instructions. Remove jars and place upside down on counter for 5 minutes. Turn right side up until cooled. As they cool, you'll hear a popping sound, indicating that internal pressure has sucked the lids tight against the jars. Check seals to ensure they are intact (lids should be indented in center). Discard any jars that are not sealed. Store up to six months.

Tomato–Peach Salsa

Makes 4 to 5 cups

2 tablespoons olive oil

4 medium tomatoes, peeled, seeded
and diced

2 peaches, peeled and diced

2 nectarines, peeled and diced

1 fresh mild green Anaheim chili,
seeded and diced

6 green onions, diced

2 garlic cloves, minced

1 tablespoon chopped fresh cilantro

1/2 teaspoon chili powder

1/4 teaspoon red pepper flakes, or to taste

Juice of 2 limes

Salt to taste

Combine all ingredients in a nonreactive bowl. Cover with plastic wrap and chill one hour before serving to blend flavors.

Serve this spicy salsa over hamburgers or use as a sauce for chicken or fish.

Fresh Raspberry Purée with
French Vanilla Ice Cream

Makes 2 cups

2 cups fresh raspberries

2 tablespoons sugar

French vanilla ice cream

Mix the raspberries and sugar together in a mixing bowl. Pass the berries through a sieve to remove seeds. Chill thoroughly. Serve sauce over ice cream.

Wine Note

LATE HARVEST WINES

"LATE HARVEST" IS A BROAD TERM ENCOMPASSING DESSERT WINES MADE FROM GRAPES ALLOWED TO RIPEN ON THE VINES LONGER THAN USUAL IN THE HOPES OF DEVELOPING "NOBLE ROT," A SOFT FUZZY MOLD THAT CAN RESULT IN EXTREMELY SWEET FRUIT. RIESLING AND SEMILLON GRAPES LEND THEMSELVES WELL TO DESSERT WINEMAKING BECAUSE OF THEIR BRIGHT FRUIT FLAVORS AND NATURALLY HIGH ACIDS.

Asian Honey-Spiced Ribs

This is a dish my kids love to wear. They find this thick, salty-sweet sauce irresistible and often eat a whole rack of ribs apiece. A rich, spicy Merlot blends into the flavors of this thick honey-sweetened sauce spiced with fresh ginger and cilantro.

WARM POTATO SALAD
page 97

ASIAN HONEY–SPICED RIBS
page 98

BAKED STUFFED APPLES WITH
LATE HARVEST WHITE RIESLING
page 99

Suggested Wine
Merlot

WARM POTATO SALAD

Serves 4

1/2 pound red potatoes, diced

1/2 pound Yellow Finn potatoes, diced

1/2 pound Purple Peruvian potatoes, diced

2 teaspoons salt

1/4 cup chopped celery

1 medium red onion, finely diced

1 teaspoon capers

1 medium dill pickle, finely diced

1 red bell pepper, finely diced

1 tablespoon chopped fresh Italian parsley

1 tablespoon chopped fresh basil

2 slices bacon, diced

2 tablespoons olive oil

2 garlic cloves, minced

2 shallots, finely diced

2 tablespoons red wine vinegar

2 tablespoons stone-ground mustard

1/4 teaspoon ground cumin

1/2 teaspoon paprika

1 teaspoon sugar

Place the diced potatoes in a large saucepan. Sprinkle with salt and cover with water. Cover and bring to a boil over high heat. Reduce the heat and simmer just until the potatoes can be pierced with a fork, about 12 minutes. Drain the potatoes in a colander and set aside to cool slightly. Place the potatoes in a large salad bowl and stir in the celery, red onion, capers, pickle, bell pepper, parsley and basil, mixing well.

Sauté the bacon over medium-high heat in a heavy skillet until golden. Remove the bacon with a slotted spoon and set on paper towels to drain. Return the skillet to the heat; add the olive oil and, when sizzling, stir in the garlic and shallots. Cook until golden, about 5 minutes. Whisk in the vinegar, mustard, cumin, paprika and sugar. Pour the hot dressing over the potato salad, mixing well. Let sit 10 minutes before serving to blend flavors.

ASIAN HONEY–SPICED RIBS

Serves 4

2 tablespoons peanut oil

1 small yellow onion, grated

3 garlic cloves, minced

1 tablespoon grated fresh ginger

1/2 cup soy sauce

2/3 cup chicken stock (see page 167)

1/4 cup Merlot

1 teaspoon dry mustard

2 tablespoons honey

2 tablespoons chopped fresh cilantro

2 tablespoons tomato paste

1/2 teaspoon Asian sesame oil

1/4 teaspoon hot chili oil

3 pounds beef or pork ribs

Salt and freshly ground black pepper
    to taste

Heat a skillet over medium-high heat. Add the peanut oil and, when hot, add the onion, garlic and ginger. Cook until the onions are soft, about 5 minutes. Add the soy sauce, chicken stock, wine, dry mustard, honey, cilantro, tomato paste, sesame oil and chili oil and simmer until thickened, about 20 minutes.

Meanwhile, preheat oven to 450°F. Place the ribs on a baking sheet and sprinkle with salt and pepper. Roast the ribs in the oven for about 20 minutes, turning once, to brown both sides. Reduce the heat to 350°F. Baste the ribs generously with the marinade; cover with aluminum foil and bake for 30 minutes. Turn and baste again. Cover the ribs again with foil and bake an additional 30 to 50 minutes, basting occasionally, until the ribs are fork-tender.

BAKED STUFFED APPLES WITH
LATE HARVEST WHITE RIESLING

Serves 4

Warm from the oven, these fragrant baked apples fill the house with a wonderful spicy aroma. Large, firm apples with a tart flavor, such as Granny Smiths, work best. To prevent discoloration, soak the peeled apples in a mixture of lemon juice and cold water.

2 apples, peeled and cut in half

1/4 cup golden raisins

1/4 cup chopped hazelnuts or walnuts

1/4 cup firmly packed brown sugar

2 tablespoons unsalted butter, softened

1/2 cup plus 1 tablespoon Late Harvest White Riesling

1/2 cup water

Preheat oven to 350°F. Scoop out the center of each apple half, forming a small cup to hold the filling. Mix together the raisins, nuts, brown sugar, butter and 1 tablespoon of the Riesling. Spoon an equal amount of filling into each apple half. Place the apples in a nonreactive baking dish fitted with a lid. Pour the water and the 1/2 cup of Riesling around the bottom of the apples. Cover and bake for 30 minutes, or until apples are tender when pierced with a fork. Uncover the apples and bake 5 to 10 minutes more, until tops are golden.

Wild Mushroom Pasta

This is one of those dishes from the Adriatic coast in which Croatian and Italian cuisines overlap. Some Mediterranean cooks finish the sauce by stirring in a tablespoon of sweet cream butter, which contributes a rich texture and mellows the flavor. This recipe calls for fresh porcini mushrooms (Boletus edulis), but I also recommend fresh chanterelles.

PENNE WITH PORCINI SAUCE
page 101

SPINACH SAUTÉ
page 102

APPLE BERRY COBBLER WITH HAZELNUT CRUMBLE
page 103

Suggested Wine
Cabernet Sauvignon

PENNE WITH PORCINI SAUCE

Serves 4

*The earthy aromas of barrel-aged Cabernet complement the
forest flavor of wild mushrooms.*

1/4 cup olive oil

1 large yellow onion, thinly sliced

1 red bell pepper, finely diced

3 garlic cloves, minced

1 pound ground veal or chicken

1 cup sliced fresh porcini or chanterelle
   mushrooms

3 medium tomatoes, chopped

2 tablespoons tomato paste

1/4 cup Merlot or other dry red wine

1/2 cup veal or chicken stock, preferably
   homemade or low-sodium canned
   (see pages 166 and 167)

2 carrots, finely grated

1/4 cup chopped fresh basil

1/4 cup chopped celery leaves

2 tablespoons chopped fresh parsley

1/4 teaspoon freshly grated nutmeg

Salt and freshly ground black pepper
   to taste

4 servings prepared penne or other pasta

1/2 cup freshly grated Parmesan cheese

Heat a heavy-bottomed saucepan over
medium heat. Add the olive oil and,
when hot, stir in the onion and bell
pepper. Cover, stirring occasionally, and
cook until the vegetables are soft, about
10 minutes. Increase the heat to medium-
high; add the minced garlic, ground veal
and mushrooms, and cook until the veal
is cooked through. Stir in the chopped
tomatoes and cook until they have softened, about 15 minutes.

Stir in the tomato paste, wine and veal
stock, blending thoroughly. Add the
grated carrots, basil, celery leaves, parsley, nutmeg, salt and pepper. Simmer the
sauce, uncovered, for at least 1 hour over
low heat, stirring occasionally. Adjust
seasonings just before serving. Spoon the
sauce liberally over cooked pasta and top
with freshly grated Parmesan cheese.

SPINACH SAUTÉ

Serves 6 to 8

3 bunches fresh spinach, stemmed

2 tablespoons olive oil

2 garlic cloves, thinly sliced

Soak the spinach in cold water. Rinse and drain in a colander, but do not dry the leaves thoroughly. Heat a large skillet over medium-high heat. Add the olive oil and, when sizzling, stir in the garlic. Sauté the garlic until it turns golden, about 1 minute. Add the spinach and cook quickly, stirring constantly, for about 3 minutes, or until the leaves are wilted.

APPLE BERRY COBBLER WITH HAZELNUT CRUMBLE

Serves 6 to 8

4 large Granny Smith apples (or other tart apples), cored, peeled and sliced

6 cups fresh or frozen blackberries

Zest of 2 oranges, finely minced

Juice of 2 oranges

Zest of 1 lemon, finely minced

Juice of 1 lemon

1/2 cup tapioca

1/4 cup all-purpose flour

2 teaspoons cinnamon

1 cup golden raisins

1 cup confectioners' sugar

Preheat oven to 350°F. Combine the apples, blackberries, orange and lemon zest and juice, tapioca, 1/4 cup flour, cinnamon, golden raisins and confectioners' sugar in a mixing bowl. Turn into an oiled 9-by-12-inch baking pan. Top with Hazelnut Crumble.

HAZELNUT CRUMBLE

1/2 cup firmly packed brown sugar

1/2 cup white sugar

11/2 cups all-purpose flour

1 cup toasted hazelnuts, chopped

3/4 cup unsalted butter, melted

Combine all the ingredients and spread evenly over the fruit mixture. Bake for about 30 minutes, or until the topping is golden and the fruit is hot and bubbling. Serve warm.

Chef's Tip

TO TOAST HAZELNUTS AND OTHER NUTS

PREHEAT OVEN TO 325°F. DISTRIBUTE SHELLED NUTS EVENLY OVER A BAKING PAN IN A SINGLE LAYER. ROAST IN THE OVEN, STIRRING OCCASIONALLY, UNTIL THE NUTS ARE GOLDEN BROWN AND FRAGRANT. MOST NUTS WILL TOAST IN ABOUT 10 MINUTES, DEPENDING ON THEIR SIZE AND VARIETY. TO REMOVE THE PAPERY SKINS FROM TOASTED HAZELNUTS, GATHER THEM IN A DISH TOWEL AND RUB BRISKLY BETWEEN LAYERS OF TOWEL.

Cabernet Grilled Sirloin

A full-flavored sirloin steak is one of my favorite cuts of meat, especially with this sauce — one that I keep adding ingredients to over the years. It creates multi-leveled layers of flavor on the palate.

MARINATED FIG AND PROSCIUTTO SALAD
page 105

CABERNET GRILLED SIRLOIN
page 106

CREAMY GARLIC POTATOES
page 107

WARM MARINATED ASPARAGUS
page 108

PEACH NAPOLEON WITH FRESH RASPBERRIES
page 109

Suggested Wines
Cabernet Sauvignon
Late Harvest White Riesling

MARINATED FIG AND PROSCIUTTO SALAD

*To blanch basil, place basil leaves in boiling water and
cook just until leaves are limp.*

½ cup whole dried figs, quartered
(substitute fresh figs when available)

1 shallot, finely chopped

⅓ cup balsamic vinegar

⅓ cup Cabernet Sauvignon

Pinch of salt

Pinch of white pepper

½ cup fresh basil leaves, blanched

2 garlic cloves

1 cup olive oil

½ pound mixed salad greens

4 long, thin slices of prosciutto

In a small sauté pan, combine the figs, shallot, vinegar, wine, salt and pepper. Bring to a simmer and cook until the volume is reduced by half. Remove from heat.

Place basil, garlic and olive oil in a blender and purée. Strain through a fine sieve or cheesecloth.

To assemble, toss the greens with the balsamic vinegar mixture, reserving the figs. Lay the prosciutto flat on a cutting board. Place a handful of the greens atop the prosciutto and roll up loosely, like a cigar. Stand this "roll" up on the salad plate and sprinkle the figs around the roll. Drizzle the basil oil mixture over all.

CABERNET GRILLED SIRLOIN

Serves 4 hungry people

To maximize flavor, I recommend serving the steaks medium-rare. Slice the steaks London Broil style — at an angle across the grain.

2 tablespoons olive oil

4 garlic cloves, minced

1 tablespoon chopped fresh Italian parsley

1 tablespoon chopped fresh rosemary

1 tablespoon chopped fresh oregano

1/2 teaspoon dry mustard

1 tablespoon soy sauce

1 tablespoon Worcestershire sauce

2 teaspoons balsamic vinegar

1/4 cup Cabernet Sauvignon

1/2 teaspoon salt

1/4 teaspoon freshly ground black pepper

1 1/2 pounds top sirloin, cut into 2 thick steaks

8 roasted shallots, chopped (see page 151)

1/2 cup beef stock

Salt and freshly ground black pepper to taste

In a large nonreactive bowl, combine the olive oil, garlic, parsley, rosemary, oregano, mustard, soy sauce, Worcestershire sauce, vinegar, wine, salt and pepper. Add the steaks and marinate for 1 hour. Meanwhile, preheat a charcoal grill. Remove the steaks from the marinade, reserving the marinade.

Transfer the reserved marinade to a saucepan and bring to a boil over high heat. Reduce heat and simmer for 10 minutes. Add the roasted shallots and beef stock. Simmer the sauce briskly until it is slightly thickened, about 5 minutes. Season with salt and pepper. Grill the steaks over medium-hot coals about 5 minutes on each side, until cooked to medium-rare (an internal temperature of 140°F). Cut the steaks into 1/4-inch-thick slices — at an angle across the grain. Drizzle sauce over the meat and pass extra sauce separately.

CREAMY GARLIC POTATOES

Serves 4

Always a favorite with guests at the winery, these creamy potatoes are seasoned with roasted garlic, fresh basil and Parmesan cheese.

8   medium new red potatoes, peeled and diced

1   garlic bulb, roasted

3   tablespoons chopped fresh basil

2   tablespoons olive oil

2   tablespoons whipping cream

2   tablespoons butter

2   tablespoons freshly grated Parmesan cheese

Salt and freshly ground black pepper to taste

Place the potatoes in a saucepan. Cover with water, salt lightly and bring to a boil over high heat. Simmer until tender. Drain the potatoes and place them in the bowl of an electric mixer. Add the roasted garlic, basil, olive oil, cream and butter. Whip the potatoes on high speed until very smooth, adding more cream if necessary. Fold in the Parmesan cheese and season with salt and pepper.

Chef's Tip

TO ROAST GARLIC

PREHEAT OVEN TO 325°F. PEEL THE DRY OUTER SKIN FROM THE GARLIC BULB. SLICE A THIN LAYER OFF THE TOP OF THE GARLIC BULB AND PLACE THE GARLIC IN AN OVENPROOF BAKING DISH. DRIZZLE WITH OLIVE OIL AND SEASON WITH SALT AND BLACK PEPPER. BAKE FOR 20 TO 30 MINUTES, UNTIL GOLDEN AND VERY SOFT. REMOVE FROM THE OVEN AND COOL. TO USE, SQUEEZE EACH GARLIC CLOVE FROM THE PEEL.

WARM MARINATED ASPARAGUS

Serves 4

*Fresh asparagus from Washington's Yakima Valley is hard to beat.
After visiting our vineyards in Eastern Washington, I often stop at a
roadside stand on my way back to the winery to pick up a case of juicy,
just-picked asparagus.*

2 tablespoons fresh lemon juice

2 tablespoons white wine vinegar

1 large shallot, minced

¼ cup olive oil

2 tablespoons Dijon mustard

½ teaspoon sugar

1 teaspoon finely chopped fresh tarragon

Dash of hot red pepper sauce

Salt and white pepper to taste

1 pound asparagus, cleaned and
   trimmed

3 cups mixed greens

1 tomato, sliced

Whisk together the lemon juice, vinegar, shallot, olive oil, mustard, sugar, tarragon, hot pepper sauce, salt and pepper in a nonreactive mixing bowl. Let stand 15 minutes to 1 hour before serving, to blend flavors. Meanwhile, steam the asparagus over high heat until tender, about 7 minutes. Distribute the greens evenly among four salad plates. Remove the asparagus from the heat and immediately toss with the dressing. Serve warm over the greens, garnished with sliced tomato.

PEACH NAPOLEON WITH FRESH RASPBERRIES

Serves 8

Feather-light, buttery puff pastry is layered with juicy peaches marinated in Late Harvest White Riesling and a creamy vanilla custard. Pour a nectar-sweet Late Harvest White Riesling to sip with this elegant dessert.

8 large egg yolks

1 cup sugar

3 cups milk or half-and-half, scalded

1/2 teaspoon vanilla

3 cups peeled and sliced ripe peaches

1/2 cup Late Harvest White Riesling

2 sheets frozen puff pastry dough

1 cup fresh raspberries or sliced strawberries

Combine the egg yolks and sugar in the top of a double boiler. Heat over 2 inches of water on medium-high heat, whisking constantly, until the eggs thicken and turn pale yellow. Gradually whisk in the scalded milk, 1/4 cup at a time. Cook, stirring constantly, until the sauce thickens and coats the back of a wooden spoon. Stir in the vanilla. If necessary, purée in a food processor or blender, or pass through a sieve to remove any lumps. Cover the sauce with plastic wrap and refrigerate until well chilled. Note: This can be prepared one day in advance.

Marinate the sliced peaches in the Late Harvest White Riesling for 30 minutes to 1 hour.

Preheat oven to 400°F. Cut the frozen puff pastry dough into 8 triangles, squares, hearts or rounds (whatever shape you like). Place the pastry on an ungreased baking sheet and bake until golden brown, about 12 to 15 minutes. Remove to a baking rack and cool to room temperature.

To assemble, pull the puff pastry squares apart in two sections, creating a top and a bottom layer. Spoon 1 tablespoon of chilled custard sauce over the bottom portion of each square. Spoon the peaches over the custard sauce, distributing evenly. Set the top portions of puff pastry on top of the peaches. Top each serving with 1 tablespoon custard sauce and spoon fresh raspberries over the top.

Suggested Wine
Late Harvest White Riesling

One-Dish Weekday Meals

One-dish meals are great fix-ahead dinners, and because of my travel schedule I often prepare them over the weekend for serving during the week. They can be served with Croatian Potato Bread or with any purchased crusty bread.

LAMB AND BEAN STEW
page 111

CROATIAN SPAGHETTI
page 112

SMOKED CHICKEN LASAGNA
page 113

WHITE BEANS WITH PUTTANESCA SAUCE
page 114

LENTIL STEW
page 115

LAMB AND BEAN STEW

Serves 6

2　tablespoons olive oil

1　pound lamb stew meat (from the shoulder or shank), cut into 1-inch cubes

1　large yellow onion, finely diced

1　red bell pepper, finely diced

1　yellow bell pepper, finely diced

1/4　cup chopped celery leaves

6　garlic cloves, minced

2　large tomatoes, cored and diced

2　tablespoons Dijon mustard

1　teaspoon dry mustard

1　teaspoon chopped fresh rosemary

1　teaspoon chopped fresh thyme

1　tablespoon chopped fresh Italian parsley

2　cups chicken stock (see page 167)

2　tablespoons Sauvignon Blanc or other dry white wine

Salt and freshly ground black pepper

1　cups pinto or navy beans, soaked overnight in cold water

Heat a large soup kettle over medium-high heat. Add the olive oil and, when sizzling, stir in the lamb, onion, red and yellow peppers, celery and garlic. Cook, stirring often, until the lamb is lightly browned and vegetables are soft, about 10 minutes. Stir in the tomatoes, Dijon mustard, dry mustard, rosemary, thyme, parsley, chicken stock and wine. Season with salt and pepper to taste. Drain the beans and add to the stew, mixing well. Cover the kettle and simmer for 1 1/2 to 2 hours, or until the meat is very tender.

Suggested Wine
Cabernet Sauvignon

Chef's Tip

PAIRING FOOD WITH RED WINE

THESE HIGHLY FLAVORED MEDITERRANEAN-STYLE DISHES GO WELL WITH ANY FULL-BODIED RED VARIETAL OR BLEND WINE. TRY MY RECOMMENDATIONS, BUT ALSO EXPERIMENT TO FIND THE WINE THAT BEST SUITS YOUR PARTICULAR TASTE WITH EACH MEAL.

CROATIAN SPAGHETTI

Serves 6

Everyone needs a great old-fashioned recipe for spaghetti. This one is a take-off on my mom's spaghetti sauce, which I could smell blocks away while walking home from school as a child.

1   1½-pound pork shoulder roast

Salt and freshly ground black pepper
   to taste

2   tablespoons olive oil

2   medium yellow onions, diced

4   garlic cloves, minced

¼ cup chopped celery leaves

1   large carrot, grated

2   16-ounce cans chopped tomatoes in
   juice, drained

1   6-ounce can tomato paste

¼ cup Cabernet Franc or other dry
   red wine

1   teaspoon sugar

½ teaspoon ground allspice

2   tablespoons chopped fresh Italian
   parsley

1   tablespoon chopped fresh basil

1   tablespoon chopped fresh oregano

6   servings prepared spaghetti

Trim the pork roast and sprinkle with salt and pepper. Heat a large, heavy saucepan over medium-high heat. Add the olive oil and, when sizzling, add the pork roast. Brown the roast well on all sides. Remove the roast and set aside. Reduce heat to medium. Add the onion, garlic, celery leaves and grated carrot. Cook until vegetables are soft, about 10 minutes. Stir in the tomatoes, tomato paste and Cabernet Franc, mixing well. Season with sugar, allspice, salt and pepper. Return the roast to the sauce. Cover and simmer 1½ hours, or until the meat is very tender and can be shredded with a fork.

Meanwhile, preheat oven to 200°F. Transfer the pork roast to a baking pan and keep warm in the oven. Add the parsley, basil and oregano to the tomato sauce and simmer 15 minutes longer. To serve, toss the tomato sauce with the prepared spaghetti. Cut the pork roast into thick slices and serve alongside the spaghetti.

Suggested Wine
Cabernet Franc

SMOKED CHICKEN LASAGNA

Serves 4 to 6

2   tablespoons olive oil

2   large onions, chopped

6   garlic cloves, chopped

1/4 cup chopped celery leaves

8   Roma tomatoes, cored and diced

1/4 cup Syrah or Pinot Noir

1   cup chicken stock (see page 167)

2   tablespoons chopped fresh Italian parsley

2   tablespoons chopped fresh basil

2   tablespoons chopped fresh oregano

1/4 cup chopped sun-dried tomatoes

1   teaspoon sugar

Salt and freshly ground black pepper to taste

6 sheets fresh pasta, trimmed to fit a 9-by-12-inch baking pan

Olive oil as needed, plus 1 tablespoon

1/2 pound portobello mushrooms, sliced

2 bunches fresh spinach, cleaned and stemmed

1 pound smoked chicken breast meat, thinly sliced

1 1/2 pounds fresh mozzarella cheese, sliced

1 cup freshly grated Parmesan cheese

Heat a skillet over medium heat. Add the olive oil and, when hot, stir in the onions. Cook until softened, about 5 minutes. Add garlic and celery leaves and cook 3 minutes more. Stir in tomatoes and simmer until very soft, 10 to 15 minutes. Add wine, chicken stock, parsley, basil, oregano, sun-dried tomatoes and sugar, mixing well. Simmer for 1/2 hour. Season with salt and pepper and set aside to cool.

Preheat oven to 350°F. Bring a large pot of salted water to a boil. Add the pasta sheets one at a time. Cook just until the pasta has softened but is still slightly resilient (al dente), about 1 1/2 minutes. Drain the pasta sheets, rub lightly with olive oil, and set aside. Meanwhile, heat a skillet over medium heat. Add the 1 tablespoon olive oil and, when hot, stir in the mushrooms. Cook until the mushrooms have softened, about 8 minutes; set aside.

To assemble: Oil a 9-by-12-inch baking pan. Spread a layer of sauce evenly over the bottom of the pan. Set a layer of lasagna noodles on top of the sauce, then cover with more sauce. Top with layers of spinach, chicken, mushrooms, and sliced cheese. Top with a layer of sauce, followed by a layer of pasta. Repeat the layers, finishing the top layer of pasta with sauce and mozzarella. Sprinkle with grated Parmesan cheese. Bake for 1 hour, or until the sauce is bubbling and hot.

Suggested Wine
Syrah

WHITE BEANS WITH PUTTANESCA SAUCE

Serves 6

*Puttanesca is actually the slang term for Italian "ladies of the night."
The story behind this sauce is that the ladies would come home tired late at
night, rummage through their kitchens and toss together this sauce made with
the ingredients they had on hand. Then they would boil up some pasta and
stir the cold sauce into the warm pasta.*

12 Roma tomatoes, cored and diced

2 tablespoons olive oil

2 tablespoons balsamic vinegar

1 bunch green onions, chopped

3 garlic cloves, minced

4 anchovy fillets, chopped (optional)

1 tablespoon capers, chopped

2 tablespoons pitted and chopped
Kalamata olives

1 tablespoon chopped fresh oregano

2 tablespoons chopped fresh basil

2 tablespoons chopped fresh Italian
parsley

1 teaspoon dry mustard

1/2 teaspoon ground cumin

Salt and freshly ground black pepper
to taste

1 pound white navy beans, cooked
according to directions on package

1/2 cup freshly grated Parmesan cheese

Combine the tomatoes, oil, vinegar, green onions, garlic, anchovies, capers, olives, oregano, basil, parsley, mustard, cumin, salt and pepper in a saucepan. Let the ingredients sit for 1 hour to blend flavors. Stir in the cooked beans. Place the saucepan over medium heat and cook until the beans are heated through. Top with grated Parmesan cheese.

Suggested Wine
Cabernet Sauvignon

LENTIL STEW

Serves 6

*The largest crop of lentils raised in the United States is grown in the
rolling hills of the Palouse region of Eastern Washington, not far from some
of our Chateau Ste. Michelle vineyards. Serve these lentils with a big
platter of fresh radishes, green onions, strips of red and yellow bell peppers,
and Croatian Potato Bread (page 43).*

1   tablespoon extra-virgin olive oil

1   large yellow onion, diced

3   garlic cloves, minced

2   large carrots, grated

1   red bell pepper, diced

2   tablespoons diced celery leaves

6   cups vegetable stock (see page 167)

1/4 cup dry white wine

1   tablespoon chopped fresh Italian
    parsley

1   tablespoon chopped fresh oregano

1/8 teaspoon ground cumin

Pinch of red pepper flakes

Salt to taste

1   pound dried green lentils, rinsed and
    sorted

Heat a skillet over medium heat. Add
the olive oil and, when hot, stir in the
onions, garlic, carrots, bell pepper and
celery leaves. Cook until the vegetables
soften, about 10 minutes. Add the vegetable stock, wine, parsley, oregano,
cumin, red pepper flakes and salt. Bring
the liquid to a boil. Stir in the lentils and
reduce heat to a simmer. Simmer, uncovered, until the lentils soften, stirring
occasionally, about 40 minutes. Serve
warm in preheated bowls.

Suggested Wine
Merlot

Braised Short Ribs in Cabernet Sauce

Lamb with Ginger–Merlot Sauce

This dish reflects the popular cooking style of fusing Pacific Rim flavors and cooking techniques with European culinary traditions. It was inspired by one of my recent trips to the Raffles Hotel in Singapore and the Regent Hotel in Bangkok.

ROMAINE WITH GARLIC MUSTARD DRESSING
page 119

LAMB WITH GINGER–MERLOT SAUCE
page 120

GRILLED GARLIC BASIL TOMATOES
page 121

FLATTENED POTATOES
page 122

POACHED PEARS WITH FIGS AND NUTS
page 123

Suggested Wines

Merlot

Late Harvest White Riesling

or

Late Harvest Semillon

Romaine with Garlic Mustard Dressing

Serves 4

3 tablespoons extra-virgin olive oil

2 teaspoons red wine vinegar

2 garlic cloves, minced

1 tablespoon finely chopped fresh basil

1/4 teaspoon dry mustard

1/8 teaspoon freshly cracked black pepper

Salt to taste

1 head romaine lettuce, washed, dried and torn into large pieces

Whisk the olive oil, vinegar, garlic, basil, dry mustard, pepper and salt in a large salad bowl. Add the lettuce. Just before serving, toss to coat leaves thoroughly.

Wine Note

BREATHING AND DECANTING

WHILE MOST WHITE WINES ARE SERVED STRAIGHT FROM THE BOTTLE, MANY FULL-BODIED AND AGED RED WINES BENEFIT FROM AERATION, OR BREATHING, WHICH ALLOWS THE LUSCIOUS AROMAS IN BIG RED WINES TO BLOSSOM AND ANY "OFF" SCENTS TO DISSIPATE. YOU CAN LET WINE BREATHE BY SIMPLY UNCORKING THE BOTTLE AN HOUR OR SO BEFORE SERVING. OLDER RED WINES OFTEN DEVELOP SEDIMENT OVER TIME. THESE WINES SHOULD ALWAYS BE DECANTED BEFORE SERVING.

LAMB WITH GINGER–MERLOT SAUCE

Serves 4

2 tablespoons olive oil

2 garlic cloves, minced

1/2 teaspoon salt

1/2 teaspoon freshly ground black pepper

8 lamb loin chops, 1/2 inch thick

In a large mixing bowl, combine the olive oil, garlic, salt and pepper. Add the lamb chops, coating well. Let marinate for 45 minutes to 1 hour at room temperature, stirring occasionally. Meanwhile, preheat a charcoal grill.

GINGER–MERLOT SAUCE

1 tablespoon peanut oil

1 tablespoon butter

2 large shallots, finely chopped

2 garlic cloves, minced

1 tablespoon grated fresh ginger

1/2 cup beef stock

1/2 cup Merlot

1/2 teaspoon dry mustard

1 tablespoon honey

1 tablespoon tomato paste

1 tablespoon soy sauce

Juice of 1/2 orange

1/4 cup chopped fresh cilantro

2 green onions, thinly sliced

Heat a skillet over medium heat. Add the peanut oil and butter and, when sizzling, stir in the shallots, garlic and ginger. Cook until the shallots are soft, about 5 minutes. Stir in the stock, wine, mustard, honey, tomato paste, soy sauce and orange juice. Simmer the mixture over low heat until reduced by a third and slightly thickened, about 15 minutes.

Grill the chops over hot coals about 4 minutes on each side, or until cooked medium-rare (to an internal temperature of 140°F).

Place 2 lamb chops on each serving plate and top with Ginger-Merlot Sauce. Sprinkle lamb chops with chopped cilantro and sliced green onions.

GRILLED GARLIC BASIL TOMATOES

Serves 4

If you don't have a grill, you can broil these garlicky tomatoes 6 inches from the heat for about 8 minutes, until the garlic turns golden and the tomatoes are heated through.

2 tablespoons olive oil

4 large ripe tomatoes, stemmed and sliced in half horizontally

2 garlic cloves, minced

Salt and freshly ground black pepper to taste

2 tablespoons chopped fresh basil

Preheat a grill to high. Spread the olive oil evenly over the tomatoes. Top with garlic and season with salt and pepper. Grill the tomatoes, cut side down, for 2 minutes. Turn and grill skin side down for another 2 minutes. Serve warm, sprinkled with fresh basil.

FLATTENED POTATOES

Serves 4

I use the bottom of a heavy skillet to "whack" these parboiled potatoes and flatten them slightly. After rubbing the potatoes with olive oil and garlic, I grill them over medium coals until their edges turn crisp and golden brown.

8 medium red potatoes

1/2 teaspoon salt

Water to cover

Waxed paper

2 tablespoons olive oil

1 garlic clove, minced

Salt and freshly ground black pepper

Preheat a charcoal grill. Pierce each potato gently with a fork. Place the potatoes in a saucepan together with the salt and enough water to cover. Bring the water to a boil. Reduce heat and simmer just until potatoes can be pierced with a fork but are still slightly undercooked. Remove from the heat at once; drain and rinse under cold running water until cooled to room temperature.

Pat the potatoes dry between paper towels. Place each potato between two sheets of waxed paper. Gently "whack" the potatoes with the bottom of a heavy skillet, just hard enough to slightly flatten the potatoes but not hard enough break them apart. Transfer the potatoes to a platter or baking sheet.

Mix together the olive oil and garlic. Rub or brush this mixture liberally over the potatoes. Sprinkle with salt and pepper. Grill the potatoes on both sides over medium coals until their edges turn golden brown, about 7 minutes per side.

POACHED PEARS WITH FIGS AND NUTS

Serves 4

Use ripe yet firm, fragrant pears for this recipe.
I recommend firm-fleshed pears such as Bartlett or Anjou.

2   large, ripe pears, peeled, halved and
    cored

2   cups cold water

1   cup Late Harvest White Riesling or
    Late Harvest Semillon

2   cloves

1   stick cinnamon

1   teaspoon grated orange zest

Combine the pears, water, wine, cloves, cinnamon and orange zest in a non-reactive saucepan. Bring to a boil over medium-high heat. Reduce heat and simmer for about 20 minutes, or until pears are soft but not mushy. Remove pears from poaching liquid with a slotted spoon, reserving 1 tablespoon poaching liquid for the fig and nut mixture.

FIGS AND NUTS

2   tablespoons unsalted butter

1/2 cup firmly packed brown sugar

1/2 cup chopped dried figs

1/2 cup chopped toasted pecans or
    walnuts (see page 103)

1   tablespoon fresh orange juice

1   tablespoon reserved poaching liquid

Melt the butter in a saucepan over medium heat. Add the brown sugar, stirring to dissolve. Stir in the figs, nuts, orange juice and reserved poaching liquid. Remove the mixture from the heat. Set a pear half on each dessert plate and top liberally with the warm figs and nuts.

Suggested Wine
Late Harvest White Riesling
or
Late Harvest Semillon

Spiedini Misti

*These hearty Italian brochettes make a festive summer dinner.
Threaded with pork, chicken, lamb and Italian sausage, the
kabobs need to marinate for at least one hour before serving and
can be prepared up to three hours in advance.*

SPIEDINI MISTI

page 125

SAFFRON RICE

page 126

GRILLED ASPARAGUS

page 127

Suggested Wine
Cabernet Franc

SPIEDINI MISTI

Serves 6

6   10-inch metal skewers

6   ounces boncless pork loin, cut into 1-inch cubes

6   ounces boneless chicken breast, cut into 1-inch cubes

6   ounces boneless lamb leg, cut into 1-inch cubes

3   Italian sausages, cut into 1-inch slices

6   slices bacon, sliced into 1-inch pieces

2   large yellow onions, quartered

24 fresh sage leaves

2   tablespoons chopped fresh Italian parsley

4   garlic cloves, minced

2   sprigs fresh rosemary, chopped

1/2 cup olive oil

4   juniper berries, crushed

Juice of 1/2 lemon

Salt and freshly ground black pepper to taste

Skewer the pork, chicken, lamb and sausage onto six skewers, alternating with pieces of bacon and onion and sage leaves. Place the skewers in a shallow nonreactive pan. Whisk together the remaining ingredients and pour over the skewers. Cover with plastic wrap and refrigerate for 1 to 3 hours.

Meanwhile, preheat a charcoal grill. Grill the kabobs over hot coals for approximately 4 minutes on each side, or until the meat is cooked through. Serve the kabobs over Saffron Rice.

Wine Note

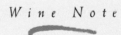

CABERNET FRANC

TRADITIONALLY USED AS A BLENDING GRAPE WITH CABERNET SAUVIGNON AND MERLOT IN CLASSIC BORDEAUX WINES, THE CABERNET FRANC RAISED IN WASHINGTON STATE HAS ENOUGH BODY AND CHARACTER TO DESERVE ITS OWN LABEL. FLAVORS AND AROMAS OF CHERRY, PLUM AND BLUEBERRY ARE ACCENTED BY GENEROUS NOTES OF SPICE AND VANILLA OAK. WELL–INTEGRATED TANNINS ADD A REFRESHING LILT TO THIS WINE.

SAFFRON RICE

Serves 6

1 tablespoon butter

1 tablespoon olive oil

1 medium onion, diced

1 fennel bulb, diced

2 garlic cloves, minced

1 cup long-grain rice

2 cups chicken stock (see page 167)

1 teaspoon grated lemon zest

Pinch of saffron threads

Heat a sauté pan with a tight-fitting lid over medium heat. Add the butter and olive oil and, when hot, stir in the onion, fennel and garlic. Cook, stirring often, until the vegetables have softened, about 10 minutes. Add the rice, mixing well. Stir in the chicken stock, lemon zest and saffron threads. Bring to a boil, then cover and reduce heat to low. Simmer slowly, without stirring, until the rice is tender and liquid is absorbed, about 20 minutes.

GRILLED ASPARAGUS

Serves 6

1 pound thick-stemmed asparagus
   (thumb-thick)

3 tablespoons extra-virgin olive oil

1 garlic clove, crushed

Freshly cracked black pepper to taste

Pinch of salt

Using a potato peeler, carefully remove only the green outer skin of the asparagus. In a small mixing bowl, combine the olive oil, garlic, a generous sprinkling of the cracked pepper and salt. Brush the asparagus liberally with this mixture. Grill the asparagus over hot coals for about 1 1/2 minutes on each side.

Chef's Tip

SELECTING ASPARAGUS

CONTRARY TO WHAT MANY PEOPLE THINK, FAT ASPARAGUS SPEARS ARE OFTEN MORE TENDER THAN SLENDER ONES. TENDERNESS HAS TO DO WITH AGE, NOT NECESSARILY SIZE, AND SKINNY SPEARS OFTEN COME FROM TIRED, OVERWORKED PLANTS. LOOK FOR THICK, HEALTHY SPEARS WITH A HIGH MOISTURE CONTENT. I USUALLY PEEL THE THICK STALKS DOWN TO THE WHITE FLESH ABOUT 1 1/2 INCHES FROM THE BASE. THIS MAKES A BEAUTIFUL PRESENTATION AND REMOVES ANY TOUGH OUTER SKIN.

Game Hens in Red Wine Sauce

This is a simple but impressive meal when served on a platter with wild rice, mushrooms and fresh herbs. When I serve this to company, the typical comment is, "John, you must have spent all day in the kitchen." I didn't.

ARUGULA WITH BALSAMIC VINAIGRETTE
page 129

CORNISH GAME HENS AND CABERNET FRANC–SAGE SAUCE
page 130

WILD RICE WITH MUSHROOMS AND HERBS
page 131

FALL ROOT CROP PURÉE WITH CHERRY CRANBERRY CHUTNEY
page 132

HAZELNUT PLUM TART
page 133

Suggested Wines
Cabernet Franc
Late Harvest White Riesling

Arugula with Balsamic Vinaigrette

Serves 4

1/2 pound fresh arugula

1 tablespoon balsamic vinegar

1 1/2 tablespoons extra-virgin olive oil

1 garlic clove, smashed

1/8 teaspoon dry mustard

Salt

Freshly ground black pepper

1/4 cup shredded Parmesan cheese

Place washed arugula in a chilled salad bowl. In a separate bowl, mix together vinegar, olive oil, garlic and mustard, then add salt and pepper to taste. Pour over the arugula and toss. Top with Parmesan cheese.

Wine Note

DEFINING THAT AROMA

OUR NOSES ARE VERY SPECIFIC WHEN IT COMES TO ANALYZING AROMAS, BUT OUR VOCABULARIES RARELY KEEP UP. TO INCREASE YOUR PLEASURE IN WINE, CHALLENGE YOURSELF TO BECOME MORE EXPLICIT. THE NEXT TIME YOU DESCRIBE AN AROMA AS "FRUITY," ASK YOURSELF: "WAS THAT BERRY, TROPICAL FRUIT OR STONE FRUIT?" IF A WINE TASTES EARTHY, DETERMINE IF THOSE FLAVORS ARE REMINISCENT OF TRUFFLES, MUSHROOMS OR EVEN FRESHLY MOWN HAY. YOU CAN PLAY THIS GAME WITH A WHOLE RANGE OF WINE AROMAS.

CORNISH GAME HENS AND
CABERNET FRANC–SAGE SAUCE

Serves 4

*Cornish game hens, or rock Cornish hens, are specially bred small chickens
that typically weigh 1½ pounds or less. Prized for their delicate, tender meat,
they are surprisingly inexpensive — perfect for entertaining on a budget.*

4   tablespoons (½ stick) unsalted butter

2   tablespoons Cabernet Franc

1   garlic clove, minced

2   large shallots, finely diced

Juice of ½ lemon

1   teaspoon dried sage

Salt and freshly ground black pepper
to taste

4   Cornish game hens

Melt the butter in a saucepan over medium heat. Add the wine, garlic, shallots, lemon juice, sage, salt and pepper. Simmer the sauce for 5 minutes.

Preheat oven to 375°F. Place the game hens in a large baking pan and baste liberally with the sauce. Bake until golden brown and tender, about 30 minutes, basting frequently. Serve one whole game hen per person.

WILD RICE WITH MUSHROOMS AND HERBS

Serves 4

2 tablespoons unsalted butter

1/2 cup sliced button mushrooms

1 small onion, diced

1 celery rib, diced

1/2 red bell pepper, diced

1 cup wild rice

1 tablespoon chopped fresh oregano

1 tablespoon chopped fresh Italian parsley

2 cups chicken stock (see page 167)

Melt the butter in a saucepan over medium heat. Stir in the mushrooms, onion, celery and bell pepper. Cook until the vegetables are soft, about 10 minutes. Add the wild rice, mixing well. Cook for 3 minutes, stirring constantly. Stir in the oregano, parsley and chicken stock. Cover and simmer until the rice is tender, 20 to 25 minutes.

Wine Note

THE SENSUAL PLEASURES OF WINE

PART OF THE PLEASURE OF WINE IS ITS AROMA, WHICH IS ENHANCED WHEN YOU TAKE THE TIME TO SWIRL IT IN THE GLASS AND SNIFF ITS BOUQUET. TO FULLY ENJOY ITS TASTE, LET IT LINGER ON THE PALATE.

FALL ROOT CROP PURÉE WITH
CHERRY CRANBERRY CHUTNEY

Serves 4

1/4 cup dried cherries, chopped

1   cup canned whole cranberries

1/4 cup loganberry or blackberry preserves

2   tablespoons orange juice

1/2 pound sweet potatoes, peeled and cut
     into chunks

1/4 pound rutabaga, peeled and cubed

1/4 pound turnips, peeled and cubed

1/4 pound Yellow Finn potatoes, peeled
     and cubed

4   cups chicken stock (see page 167)

Salt to taste

1/8 teaspoon grated orange zest

In a nonreactive bowl, mix the cherries,
cranberries, preserves and orange juice
together and let stand for 30 minutes.

In a large cooking pot, boil sweet potatoes, rutabaga, turnips and potatoes in
chicken stock until tender. Drain well
and purée in food processor. Add salt
and orange zest to blend. To serve, top
with a large dollop of chutney.

Hazelnut Plum Tart

Serves 8 (Makes one 10-inch tart)

A sweet, buttery-rich pastry, studded with ground hazelnuts, is filled with fresh plums and topped with an orange marmalade glaze.

3 cups flour

1/2 teaspoon salt

1 cup ground toasted hazelnuts (see page 103)

1/2 cup sugar

6 ounces unsalted butter, chilled and sliced

2 large eggs

Cold water, if needed

1 tablespoon unsalted butter, melted

4 cups sliced, pitted fresh plums

1/2 cup orange marmalade, heated

Combine the flour, salt, hazelnuts, sugar and chilled butter in a food processor or a mixer fitted with a dough paddle. Blend until the butter is reduced to pea-sized bits. Add the eggs, and cold water if necessary, mixing to form a stiff dough. Form the dough into a hamburger-shaped patty; wrap in plastic wrap and chill for 1 hour.

Preheat oven to 350°F. Oil a 10-inch tart pan with a removable bottom. Roll the dough out on a clean, floured surface into a 12-inch circle. Line the pan with the dough and trim edges. Brush the pastry with the melted butter. Beginning at the edges of the tart shell, arrange the sliced plums in concentric circles, overlapping slices slightly. Continue until the tart shell is filled with plum slices. Bake the tart for about 30 minutes, or until the pastry is golden. Let the tart cool for 10 minutes. Using a pastry brush, coat the plums with the heated orange marmalade. Let the tart cool 30 minutes before serving. If desired, top with whipped cream or vanilla ice cream.

Suggested Wine
Late Harvest White Riesling

Tuscan Chicken with Fresh Rosemary

I've been cooking this flavorful dish for many years, and it's still one of my favorites. With its intense flavors of wine, garlic and fresh rosemary, this dish is not for the faint of heart, nor, for that matter, is the Meritage wine.

GRILLED FETA–STUFFED GRAPE LEAVES

page 135

CAPONATA

page 136

TUSCAN CHICKEN WITH FRESH ROSEMARY

page 137

ANCHOVY AND GARLIC BRUSSELS SPROUTS

page 138

AGED CHEESES AND FRESH FRUIT WITH
LATE HARVEST WHITE RIESLING

page 139

Suggested Wine
Red Meritage

GRILLED FETA–STUFFED GRAPE LEAVES

Serves 4

12 grape leaves, packed in brine

6 thin slices prosciutto, sliced in half lengthwise

1/2 pound soft, fresh feta cheese

Freshly ground black pepper

Toothpicks for securing

2 tablespoons olive oil

Preheat a charcoal grill or indoor grill to high heat. Rinse the grape leaves in cold water; drain and blot dry with paper towels. Place one-half slice of prosciutto on each leaf. Spread 2 tablespoons of feta cheese over the prosciutto and grind some black pepper over the cheese. With the stem end of the grape leaf facing you, fold the left side of the leaf over the cheese. Repeat with the right side of the leaf. Fold the forward edge of the leaf toward the center, then roll the leaf into a cigar shape and secure with a toothpick. Rub or brush the grape leaves lightly with olive oil. Grill, turning occasionally, until lightly charred on each side, about 12 minutes total. Serve warm.

Wine Note

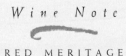

RED MERITAGE

By definition, Meritage is a wine blended from 100 percent Bordeaux grape varieties grown in the United States. Winemakers blend grapes from Cabernet Sauvignon, Cabernet Franc, Merlot, Malbec and Petite Verdot, all of which have adapted extremely well to the vineyard conditions of the Columbia Valley. Meritage is a wine that winemakers love to make because it reflects their personal tastes. Just like a chef using different ingredients, they blend red wine varietals to suit their individual taste.

CAPONATA

Makes 2 1/2 cups

Caponata keeps for up to three days in the refrigerator.
Serve warm or at room temperature.

1   medium eggplant

Salt to taste

2   tablespoons olive oil

1   large yellow onion, diced

2   garlic cloves, minced

1   red bell pepper, diced

1   yellow bell pepper, diced

1   tablespoon tomato paste mixed with
    2 tablespoons water

1/4 cup chopped pitted Kalamata olives

1   tablespoon capers

2   anchovy fillets, finely chopped

1/2 teaspoon dry mustard

1/8 teaspoon ground cumin

1   tablespoon chopped fresh oregano

1   tablespoon chopped fresh basil

1   tablespoon chopped fresh Italian
    parsley

1   tablespoon balsamic vinegar

1   51/2-ounce can albacore tuna, drained

1   baguette, thinly sliced

Olive oil, as needed

Peel the eggplant and dice into 1/2-inch cubes. Place the eggplant in a colander, sprinkle with salt and let drain for 15 minutes. Blot the eggplant dry on paper towels and set aside. Heat a large sauce pan over medium-high heat. Add the olive oil and, when sizzling, stir in the onion, garlic, and red and yellow peppers. Cook until softened, about 5 minutes. Add the eggplant and cook, stirring often, until softened, about 10 minutes. Stir in the tomato paste mixed with water.

Remove from the heat and stir in the olives, capers, anchovies, dry mustard, cumin, oregano, basil, parsley, vinegar, tuna and salt to taste, mixing well. Transfer to a serving bowl. Meanwhile, preheat a broiler. Brush the baguette slices lightly with olive oil. Place on a baking sheet and broil until lightly golden. Spread Caponata generously over the baguette slices and transfer to a serving platter.

TUSCAN CHICKEN WITH FRESH ROSEMARY

Serves 4

With the flavor of fresh rosemary and the distinctive taste of grilled food, the complex nature of a fine Meritage is the perfect complement to this dish.

1 large fryer chicken, divided into
  8 pieces

Salt and freshly ground black pepper

2 tablespoons olive oil

1 medium yellow onion, finely diced

3 garlic cloves, minced

1 tablespoon tomato paste

1 cup diced tomatoes

1 cup Red Meritage or other dry
  red wine

2 4-inch sprigs fresh rosemary

1 clove

1 bay leaf

Salt and freshly ground black pepper
  to taste

4 servings prepared spaghettini

2 tablespoons olive oil

2 tablespoons minced fresh Italian
  parsley

1/4 cup freshly grated Parmesan cheese

Sprinkle the chicken pieces liberally with salt and pepper. Heat a large skillet over medium-high heat. Add the olive oil and, when sizzling, add the chicken pieces. Cook, turning occasionally, until golden brown on all sides. Transfer chicken to a platter and set aside.

Return the skillet to the heat. Stir in the onion and garlic and cook, stirring often, for about 5 minutes, or until softened. Stir in the tomato paste, mixing well. Add the tomatoes, wine, rosemary sprigs, clove and bay leaf. When the mixture comes to a boil, add the chicken pieces. Reduce the heat to a simmer. Cover and cook for 30 minutes, turning chicken occasionally. Remove the lid and simmer uncovered for 5 minutes to thicken the sauce. Season with salt and pepper.

To serve, toss the prepared spaghettini with olive oil and season with salt and pepper. Serve alongside the chicken and sprinkle with parsley and grated Parmesan cheese.

ANCHOVY AND GARLIC BRUSSELS SPROUTS

Serves 4

Brussels sprouts are one of the few vegetables whose flavor improves after a fall or winter frost. If you have access to a farmer's market, look for brussels sprouts left on the stem. This way, you're assured of freshness.

1 pound brussels sprouts, ends and any brown leaves trimmed

1 1/2 tablespoons extra-virgin olive oil

1 tablespoon balsamic vinegar

1 tablespoon red wine vinegar

1 garlic clove, minced

2 anchovy fillets, finely chopped

1/8 teaspoon dry mustard

1/2 teaspoon freshly ground black pepper

1/4 teaspoon sugar

Salt to taste

Place the brussels sprouts in a skillet with a steamer basket and a tight-fitting lid. Fill the pan with 1 inch of water. Cover and bring to a boil over high heat. Reduce heat to medium and steam until brussels sprouts can be easily pierced with a fork, about 10 minutes. Remove the sprouts from the heat and keep warm. Meanwhile, whisk together the remaining ingredients. Transfer the brussels sprouts to a serving dish and pour the sauce over the sprouts, mixing well.

AGED CHEESES AND FRESH FRUIT WITH LATE HARVEST WHITE RIESLING

Serves 4

1 Golden Delicious apple, cored and sliced

1 Red Delicious apple, cored and sliced

1 Bartlett pear, cored and sliced

1 Anjou pear, cored and sliced

Lemon or juice of ½ lemon

4 ounces English Stilton cheese

4 ounces Brie cheese

4 ounces sharp English Cheddar cheese

Rub a slice of lemon over the surface of each fruit slice to keep from browning. Or, place the fruit slices in a bowl of 1 quart cold water mixed with the juice of ½ lemon for just a few minutes — this will also prevent apples and pears from browning. Arrange fruit slices and cheeses on a serving tray. Serve with a chilled Late Harvest White Riesling.

Braised Rabbit with Cherries

This is a recipe that I created while filming my television show
in Provence. It's a typical country-style Mediterranean dish
made with rabbit and fresh cherries. I can still remember going
to the open-air market in Ste. Remy on a warm spring
afternoon and purchasing the ingredients. Rabbit is a specialty
in the Mediterranean, but it's often overlooked in the States.
It has a wonderful flavor that I can't quite describe,
but trust me — you'll like it.

CRISP ROMAINE AND FRESH HERB SALAD

page 141

BRAISED RABBIT WITH CHERRIES

page 142

PASTA AND PROSCIUTTO

page 143

Suggested Wine
Red Meritage

CRISP ROMAINE AND FRESH HERB SALAD

1 tablespoon red wine vinegar

1 tablespoon balsamic vinegar

2 tablespoons extra-virgin olive oil

1 teaspoon chopped fresh basil

1 teaspoon chopped fresh oregano

1 teaspoon chopped fresh Italian parsley

Pinch of sugar

Salt and freshly ground pepper to taste

1 head romaine lettuce, rinsed and dried

Mix together the vinegars, olive oil, basil, oregano, parsley, sugar, salt and pepper. Tear the lettuce leaves into bite-size pieces. Place in a salad bowl and toss with the dressing.

Chef's Tip

FOOD AND WINE PAIRING

FRESH CHERRIES FROM EASTERN WASHINGTON HAVE A NATURAL AFFINITY FOR OUR MERITAGE WINES, PRODUCED IN THE SAME REGION. THESE ROBUST WINES ARE PACKED WITH CONCENTRATED FLAVORS AND AROMAS OF DARK CHERRY, WITH NOTES OF COFFEE, MINT, OAK AND SPICE THAT HIGHLIGHT THE CHERRIES AND HERBS IN THIS DISH.

BRAISED RABBIT WITH CHERRIES

Serves 4

2	tablespoons olive oil
1	3- to 4-pound rabbit, divided into quarters
1	large yellow onion, finely diced
1	red bell pepper, finely diced
1	yellow bell pepper, finely diced
2	large tomatoes, cored and diced
4	garlic cloves, minced
1	cup Merlot
1	cup Bing cherries, pitted and halved
1	tablespoon balsamic vinegar
2	tablespoons chopped celery leaves
2	tablespoons chopped fresh Italian parsley
1	tablespoon chopped fresh rosemary
1	tablespoon chopped fresh thyme
1	bay leaf
2	teaspoons dry mustard
1	teaspoon grated lemon zest

Heat a heavy skillet over medium-high heat. Add the olive oil and, when sizzling, add the rabbit. Brown the rabbit pieces on both sides. Remove the rabbit from the pan and set aside. Stir in the onions and peppers and simmer until the vegetables have softened, about 10 minutes. Stir in the tomatoes, garlic and Merlot. Simmer the sauce, uncovered, for about 15 minutes, or until reduced by a third.

Stir in the cherries, vinegar, celery leaves, parsley, rosemary, thyme, bay leaf, dry mustard and lemon zest. Return the rabbit to the pot. Cover and simmer for 45 minutes.

PASTA AND PROSCIUTTO

Serves 4

1 large onion, sliced thin, julienned

1/4 cup chopped prosciutto (2 pieces chopped bacon may be substituted)

3 garlic cloves, mashed

2 tablespoons olive oil

1 cup chopped Roma tomatoes

1/2 cup chicken stock (see page 167)

2 tablespoons Sauvignon Blanc

Pinch of red pepper flakes

Generous amount of freshly ground black pepper

1/4 cup fresh chopped basil

1 pound wide noodle pasta, cooked al dente (see page 29)

1/4 cup Parmesan cheese, grated

In a large sauté pan over medium-high heat, sauté onion, prosciutto and garlic in olive oil. Cook until very soft and slightly browned. Add tomatoes and stir. Add chicken stock, wine, pepper flakes and pepper. Cover and simmer over low heat until sauce-like, about 15 minutes. Stir in basil and serve over the pasta. Garnish with Parmesan cheese.

Wine Note

THE GLASS MENAGERIE

CUSTOM RATHER THAN RULE LINKS PARTICULAR GLASS SHAPES TO CERTAIN WINES. OVER THE CENTURIES, EACH WINE REGION DEVELOPED A PARTICULAR STYLE OF GLASS IN THE BELIEF THAT IT REFLECTED SOME OF THE FINER QUALITIES OF THEIR WINES. NOW THAT WE IMPORT A FAR WIDER RANGE OF WINES FROM AROUND THE GLOBE, AN ALL—PURPOSE GLASS IS ALMOST A NECESSITY — AND A WONDERFUL SOLUTION. LOOK FOR A CLEAR, STEMMED GLASS WITH A BOWL LARGE ENOUGH TO HOLD 3 TO 4 OUNCES OF WINE WHEN FILLED TO ONE—THIRD CAPACITY. THIS ALLOWS ENOUGH ROOM FOR SWIRLING THE WINE AND SNIFFING THE BOUQUET. A GLASS WITH A SMALLER OPENING AT THE TOP OF THE BOWL WILL HELP CON-CENTRATE THE WINE'S AROMA, AND A THIN, ELEGANT STEM AND LIP WILL SIMPLY ADD TO YOUR ENJOYMENT.

Autumn Braised Short Ribs

*During the chilly months of fall and winter, I love cooking
dishes that simmer for a long time, filling the house with fragrant
aromas. In this recipe — my father's all-time favorite —
beef ribs cook slowly with wine and other aromatic elements,
producing a succulent, full-flavored dish that blends wonderfully
with Cabernet Sauvignon. The brisk tannins of a young Cabernet
balance the rich, meaty ribs, keeping the palate refreshed.*

ANTIPASTO WITH CABERNET VINAIGRETTE

page 145

BRAISED SHORT RIBS IN CABERNET SAUCE

page 146

APPLE AND PEAR SORBET

page 147

Suggested Wines
Cabernet Sauvignon
Late Harvest White Riesling

Antipasto with Cabernet Vinaigrette

CABERNET VINAIGRETTE

1 cup Cabernet Sauvignon

1 tablespoon balsamic vinegar

1/2 teaspoon Worcestershire sauce

1/2 clove garlic, minced

1/2 cup extra-virgin olive oil

1 tablespoon chopped fresh oregano

1 tablespoon chopped fresh marjoram

2 tablespoons chopped fresh Italian parsley

1 teaspoon dry mustard

1/2 teaspoon sugar

1/2 teaspoon freshly ground black pepper

Salt

Heat the wine in a small saucepan over high heat. When it comes to a boil, reduce heat and simmer until the wine is reduced by half, about 12 minutes. Stir in the vinegar, Worcestershire sauce and garlic. Simmer about 5 minutes, or until the garlic has softened. Transfer the mixture to a nonreactive bowl; cool to room temperature. (To quicken chilling, place in the refrigerator.) When the wine mixture is cool, whisk in the olive oil, oregano, marjoram, parsley, dry mustard, sugar and pepper. Season to taste with salt.

ANTIPASTO

1 head butter lettuce, rinsed and dried

1 head red leaf lettuce, rinsed and dried

1 red bell pepper, roasted and sliced (see page 39)

1 yellow bell pepper, roasted and sliced

1 small fennel bulb, thinly sliced

1 small white onion, thinly sliced

1 medium zucchini, thinly sliced

1 cup freshly grated Asiago cheese

1/2 cup Greek olives, pitted and sliced

Tear the lettuce into bite-size pieces into a large salad bowl. Add the roasted peppers, fennel, onion, zucchini, cheese and olives. Toss with the Cabernet Vinaigrette just before serving.

BRAISED SHORT RIBS IN CABERNET SAUCE

Serves 6

3   pounds beef short ribs, separated

Flour for dredging

2   tablespoons olive oil

3   slices bacon, diced

1   large yellow onion, thinly sliced

3   garlic cloves, minced

1   cup Roma tomatoes, chopped

1   carrot, grated

1 – 2 tablespoons tomato paste

2   tablespoons chopped celery leaves

2   tablespoons chopped fresh Italian
    parsley

1/2 tablespoon fresh rosemary

1   tablespoon chopped fresh thyme

1   tablespoon dry mustard

1   clove

Pinch of sugar

Pinch of grated orange zest

1 1/2 cups Cabernet Sauvignon

Salt and freshly ground pepper to taste

Preheat oven to 375°F. Dredge the short ribs in flour. Heat a Dutch oven or large heavy pot with a fitted lid over medium-high heat. Add the olive oil. When hot, add the short ribs and brown on all sides. Remove the short ribs and set aside. Add the bacon, onion and garlic. Cook until the onions are tender and the bacon is golden on the edges, about 10 minutes.

Stir in the tomatoes and grated carrot; cook until softened. Stir in the tomato paste, celery leaves, parsley, rosemary, thyme, dry mustard, clove, sugar, orange zest, Cabernet Sauvignon, salt and pepper, mixing well. Put the short ribs back in the pot; cover and place in the oven. Cook for about 1 hour, stirring occasionally, until the meat is very tender. Distribute the ribs among serving bowls or plates. Ladle sauce generously over the ribs.

Apple and Pear Sorbet

Serves 6

Pears and apples are natural complements to the honeyed sweetness of a Late Harvest White Riesling. Make this frosty dessert a day ahead of time and serve with a glass of Late Harvest White Riesling on the side.

3 Golden Delicious apples (or other sweet apples), peeled, cored and sliced

3 Anjou pears (other ripe pears can be substituted), peeled, cored and sliced

1 tablespoon fresh lemon juice

¼ cup sugar

2 tablespoons Late Harvest White Riesling

Purée all of the ingredients in a blender or food processor. Transfer the mixture to an ice cream machine and prepare according to manufacturer's directions (or see directions below). Keep frozen until ready to serve.

If you don't have an ice cream or gelato machine, freeze the sorbet mixture in a shallow tray, stirring with a whisk every hour until frozen. This incorporates air and breaks up ice crystals.

Halibut with Roasted Shallot–Pinot Sauce

This is a great menu for breaking the food and wine rules that prohibit red wine with white fish.

SMOKED CHICKEN CROSTINI WITH SUN–DRIED TOMATO
PASTE AND ROASTED GARLIC MAYONNAISE

page 149

GARDEN SALAD

page 150

HALIBUT WITH ROASTED SHALLOT–PINOT SAUCE

page 151

HERBED NEW POTATOES

page 152

STRAWBERRY TRIFLE

page 153

Suggested Wines
Pinot Noir
Late Harvest White Riesling

SMOKED CHICKEN CROSTINI WITH SUN–DRIED TOMATO PASTE AND ROASTED GARLIC MAYONNAISE

Serves 10 as an appetizer

You'll need roasted garlic and roasted red pepper for this recipe, so plan ahead. Both the Roasted Garlic Mayonnaise and Sun-Dried Tomato Paste can be prepared up to two days ahead.

ROASTED GARLIC MAYONNAISE

4 garlic cloves, roasted (see page 107)

1/2 cup mayonnaise

1 teaspoon Dijon mustard

Place the roasted garlic cloves in a mixing bowl and mash with a fork. Stir in the mayonnaise and Dijon mustard, mixing well.

SUN–DRIED TOMATO PASTE

1/4 cup olive oil

1/2 cup reconstituted dried tomatoes

Pinch of salt

Place all the ingredients in a blender or food processor and purée.

CROSTINI

1 baguette, thinly sliced and toasted

2 smoked boneless chicken breasts (approximately 3 ounces each), julienned

1/4 cup chopped fresh cilantro

To assemble Crostini, spread Roasted Garlic Mayonnaise on each crostino. Top with slices of smoked chicken, followed by a teaspoon of Sun-Dried Tomato Paste. Sprinkle with chopped cilantro.

GARDEN SALAD

Serves 4

2　heads Bibb lettuce, washed and dried

1　head red leaf lettuce, washed and dried

1　red onion, thinly sliced

1　cucumber, thinly sliced

1　teaspoon sugar

2　tablespoons red wine vinegar

3　tablespoons extra-virgin olive oil

Salt and freshly ground black pepper
　　to taste

Tear the lettuce into bite-size pieces and place in a large salad bowl together with the sliced onion and cucumber. Sprinkle with the sugar, vinegar and olive oil and toss lightly. Season to taste with salt and pepper.

HALIBUT WITH ROASTED SHALLOT–PINOT SAUCE

Serves 4

2 large garlic cloves, minced

2 tablespoons extra-virgin olive oil

1/8 teaspoon chopped fresh thyme

2 teaspoons fresh lemon juice

Salt and ground white pepper to taste

4 5 ounce halibut fillets

2 teaspoons unsalted butter

6 roasted shallots

1 cup Pinot Noir

1/4 cup fish or chicken stock (see pages 166 and 167)

2 tablespoons balsamic vinegar

2 tablespoons unsalted butter, chilled and cut into 8 pieces

Fresh thyme leaves and minced red bell pepper for garnish

Preheat a charcoal grill. Mix together the garlic, olive oil, thyme, lemon juice, salt and pepper. Rub this mixture over the halibut fillets. Let the fillets sit 15 minutes before grilling.

Melt the 2 teaspoons butter in a saucepan over medium heat. Add the roasted shallots and cook for 2 minutes. Increase the heat to medium-high. Add the Pinot Noir, fish stock and balsamic vinegar. Simmer the sauce briskly, until it is reduced by a third. Reduce the heat to low. With a whisk, blend in the chilled butter, one bit at a time, until the butter is incorporated and the sauce is smooth and glossy. Remove the sauce from the heat. Serve at once, or keep warm in a preheated Thermos-type container.

Grill the halibut over medium-hot coals about 3 minutes per side, or until the fish is just cooked through and is no longer translucent in the center. Spoon a pool of sauce onto each plate and set the halibut fillets in the center of the sauce. Garnish with fresh thyme leaves and minced bell pepper.

Chef's Tip

TO ROAST SHALLOTS

PREHEAT OVEN TO 350°F. TRIM BOTH ENDS OF THE SHALLOTS AND SET THEM ON A SHEET OF ALUMINUM FOIL. SPRINKLE THE SHALLOTS WITH OLIVE OIL. WRAP THEM IN THE FOIL AND SEAL TIGHTLY ON BOTH ENDS. BAKE FOR 30 MINUTES, OR UNTIL SHALLOTS ARE VERY SOFT. TO USE, REMOVE THE SKIN AND SLICE THE SHALLOTS IN HALF.

HERBED NEW POTATOES

Serves 4

8 small new red potatoes

1/2 tablespoon chopped fresh Italian parsley

1/2 tablespoon chopped fresh basil

2 tablespoons olive oil

Salt and freshly ground black pepper to taste

Cook potatoes in lightly salted water until the potatoes are tender, about 12 minutes. Drain and place potatoes on serving platter or plate. Drizzle olive oil over potatoes. Add salt and pepper. Garnish with the parsley and basil.

Strawberry Trifle

Serves 4

3 1-inch-thick slices pound cake, cut into 1-inch cubes

1/4 cup Whidbey's Loganberry Liqueur

1/2 pound sliced fresh strawberries

2 cups whipping cream, whipped and lightly sweetened

Sprinkle the pound cake with the liqueur. Layer the pound cake with the strawberries and whipped cream in wine glasses or goblets, making three layers in each glass. Chill for at least 15 minutes and up to 3 hours before serving.

Suggested Wine

Late Harvest White Riesling

Chef's Tip

STORE-BOUGHT VS. HOMEMADE CAKE

YOU'LL NEED THREE SLICES OF POUND CAKE FOR THIS RECIPE, SO PLAN AHEAD. NOTHING BEATS A HOMEMADE POUND CAKE OR ANGEL FOOD CAKE, BUT THERE ARE WONDERFUL STORE-BOUGHT ALTERNATIVES THAT MAKE THE REST OF THIS RECIPE QUICK AND EASY, WITH NO COMPROMISE IN TASTE. I RECOMMEND USING WHIDBEY'S LOGANBERRY LIQUEUR, BUT GRAND MARNIER MAKES A DELICIOUS SUBSTITUTE.

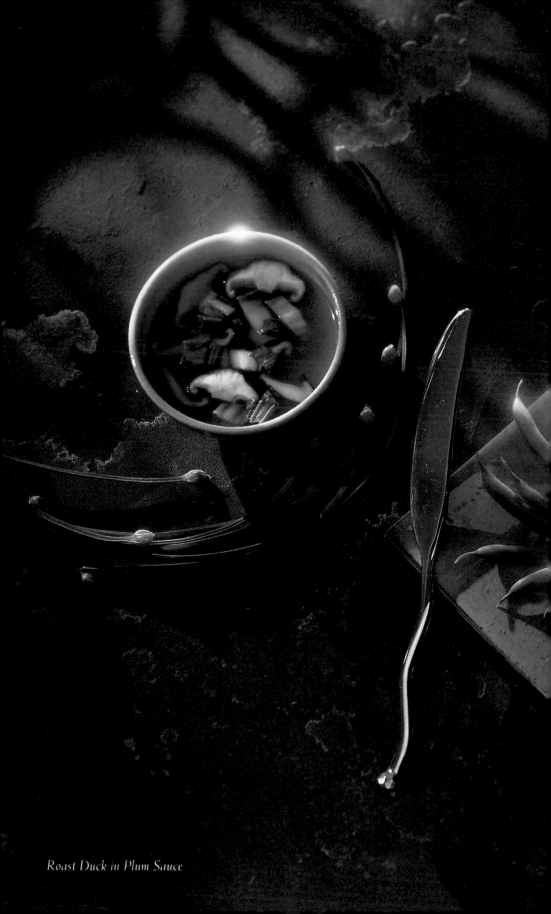

Roast Duck in Plum Sauce

Mediterranean Couscous

This is one of my favorite dishes to make when I'm entertaining a crowd. The colorful sauce can be prepared up to one day in advance and reheated just before serving.

MEDITERRANEAN SALAD
page 157

MEDITERRANEAN COUSCOUS WITH
CHICKEN, LAMB AND PORK
page 158

FRESH FRUIT IN LATE HARVEST WHITE RIESLING
page 159

Suggested Wines
Syrah
Late Harvest White Riesling

Mediterranean Salad

Serves 4

1 cucumber, sliced into rounds or cubed

2 medium tomatoes, cut into wedges

1/4 cup whole pitted Greek olives

1 red onion, sliced into rings

1 tablespoon chopped fresh basil

1 tablespoon chopped fresh Italian parsley

1 garlic clove, mashed

2 tablespoons extra-virgin olive oil

2 tablespoons red wine vinegar

Salt and freshly ground black pepper to taste

Toss all the ingredients together in a nonreactive bowl. Let sit 15 minutes before serving to blend flavors.

Wine Note

SYRAH

WIDELY PLANTED IN FRANCE'S RHONE VALLEY AND IN CALIFORNIA, WHERE GROWERS HAVE BEEN DUBBED THE "RHONE RANGERS," SYRAH IS NOW PLANTED IN WASHINGTON'S COLUMBIA VALLEY, TOO. BRIMMING WITH VIGOROUS FRUIT, THESE GENEROUS, SPICY RED WINES OFTEN HAVE AN ENTICING SMOKY QUALITY. THIS GRAPE IS ALSO GROWN IN AUSTRALIA, WHERE IT IS CALLED SHIRAZ.

COUSCOUS

COUSCOUS HAS BEEN A MEDITERRANEAN CULINARY TRADITION FOR AT LEAST A THOUSAND YEARS. IT IS A FORM OF PASTA MADE FROM GRAINS OF SEMOLINA FLOUR. TRADITIONALLY, PREPARATION OF COUSCOUS WAS A LENGTHY PROCESS: GRINDING RAW WHEAT, THEN HAND–RUBBING THE FLOUR INTO TINY GRAINS.

MEDITERRANEAN COUSCOUS WITH CHICKEN, LAMB AND PORK

Serves 6

2 tablespoons olive oil

1 pound lamb shoulder, cut into 1-inch cubes

1 pound pork shoulder, cut into 1-inch cubes

6 chicken thighs, boned and cut into 1-inch cubes

1 large onion, diced

1 fennel bulb, sliced

1 red bell pepper, sliced

1 yellow bell pepper, sliced

1/4 cup chopped celery leaves

6 garlic cloves, minced

1/4 cup Sauvignon Blanc

2 cups chicken stock (see page 167)

6 Roma tomatoes, cored and diced

2 tablespoons tomato paste

1 tablespoon chopped fresh Italian parsley

1 tablespoon chopped fresh oregano

1 teaspoon ground coriander

1 teaspoon ground cumin

Salt and freshly ground black pepper

Pinch of red pepper flakes

1 10-ounce package couscous

Preheat oven to 325°F. Heat a large soup pot or Dutch oven over medium-high heat. Add the olive oil and, when hot, stir in the lamb, pork and chicken. Cook, stirring often, until the meat is well browned. Remove the meat from the pot and set aside. Drain the excess oil from the cooking pot, reserving 1 tablespoon. Return the pot to the heat. When hot, stir in the onion, fennel, peppers, celery leaves and garlic. Cook, stirring often, until the vegetables are tender, about 7 minutes. Stir in the wine, chicken stock and diced tomatoes. Simmer until the tomatoes are very soft, about 10 minutes.

Stir in the tomato paste, parsley, oregano, coriander, cumin, salt and pepper to taste and red pepper flakes. When the sauce comes to a simmer, add the browned lamb, pork and chicken. Cover the pot and bake in the preheated oven for 45 minutes, or until the meat is very tender. Serve over prepared couscous.

FRESH FRUIT IN LATE HARVEST WHITE RIESLING

Serves 4

Spiced with fresh ginger and bathed in a honey-sweet Late Harvest White Riesling, this refreshing fruit dessert is elegant in its simplicity. Look for perfectly ripe fruit that feels heavy in your hand and emits sweet, fragrant aromas. Rather than following this recipe exactly, use whatever fruits are in season. For example, you could substitute ripe blackberries for the cherries, or fresh strawberries for the nectarines. This looks beautiful served in long-stemmed wine glasses.

2 ripe peaches, peeled and sliced

1 ripe nectarine, sliced

5 ripe plums, sliced

1 cup pitted sweet cherries

1 tablespoon grated fresh ginger

Juice of 1/4 lemon

1 cup Late Harvest White Riesling

4 sprigs fresh mint, for garnish

In a nonreactive bowl, toss together the peaches, nectarines, plums, cherries, ginger and lemon juice. Distribute the fruit evenly among four wine glasses or serving bowls. Top each serving with 1/4 cup Late Harvest White Riesling. Chill thoroughly. Garnish with fresh mint.

Asian Duck in Plum Sauce

*This is another example of East meets West flavors.
I tasted a similar dish in Singapore, and it was the first to
make me aware of how deliciously some red wines pair with
spicy Asian foods.*

SHIITAKE MUSHROOM SOUP
page 161

GINGER CUCUMBER SALAD
page 162

ROAST DUCK IN PLUM SAUCE
page 163

CHICKEN–SEASONED SAIFUN NOODLES
page 164

FRENCH VANILLA ICE CREAM WITH
CHOCOLATE, COFFEE AND LOGANBERRY TOPPING
page 165

Suggested Wine

Merlot

SHIITAKE MUSHROOM SOUP

Serves 4

2 tablespoons peanut oil

1/4 teaspoon Asian sesame oil

1/8 teaspoon hot chili oil

1 medium yellow onion, finely diced

1 garlic clove, minced

1 tablespoon grated fresh ginger

1/4 pound fresh shiitake mushrooms, sliced

1 small head bok choy, chopped

5 cups chicken or veal stock (see pages 166 and 167)

1/4 cup Dry Riesling or other dry white wine

2 tablespoons soy sauce

Heat a skillet over medium-high heat. Add the peanut oil, sesame oil and chili oil. When the oils are sizzling, stir in the onion, garlic and ginger. Cook 5 minutes, or until the onions soften. Stir in the mushrooms and bok choy. Cook just until the vegetables have softened, about 5 minutes. Stir in the stock, wine and soy sauce. Cook for 5 more minutes, stirring often. Serve hot.

GINGER CUCUMBER SALAD

Serves 6

*Use English cucumbers in this dish. Also known as seedless or European
cucumbers, they are thin-skinned and virtually seedless. If you can't locate
English cucumbers, I recommend peeling and seeding regular cucumbers.*

1   English cucumber, unpeeled, sliced in
thin rounds

1   cup seasoned rice wine vinegar, or
regular rice wine vinegar mixed with
2 teaspoons sugar

1   tablespoon chopped pickled ginger

1/2 medium white onion, minced

Pinch of salt

Chopped fresh cilantro, for garnish

Toss the cucumber, vinegar, ginger,
onion and salt together in a nonreactive
bowl. Cover and marinate in the refrigerator at least one hour, or overnight.
Garnish with cilantro.

ROAST DUCK IN PLUM SAUCE

Serves 4

1 tablespoon olive oil

2 duck breasts, divided in halves

1 fennel bulb, thinly sliced

1 large yellow onion, thinly sliced

2 garlic cloves, minced

2 tablespoons grated fresh ginger

2 large tomatoes, cored and diced

2 teaspoons tomato paste

1/2 teaspoon dry mustard

2 teaspoons rice wine vinegar

1 tablespoon soy sauce

1 cup pitted and sliced fresh plums
   (or Italian prunes)

1/2 cup Merlot

1 tablespoon honey

Pinch of red pepper flakes

Heat a heavy skillet over medium heat. Add the olive oil and, when hot, add the duck breasts, skin side down. Cook the duck breasts until the skin turns golden and the fat is rendered out. Remove the duck breasts from the pan and set aside. Pour off excess oil, reserving 1 tablespoon.

Return the skillet to the heat. Stir in the fennel, onion, garlic and ginger. Cook, stirring often, until the vegetables are very soft, about 15 minutes. Add the tomatoes and cook until softened, about 10 minutes. Stir in the tomato paste, mustard, rice wine vinegar, soy sauce, sliced plums, wine, honey and red pepper flakes. Simmer until the plums are soft, about 12 minutes.

Return the duck breasts to the skillet; cover and simmer for 20 minutes, or until the duck breasts are cooked through.

To serve, cut each duck breast into 1/2-inch slices and fan out on a serving plate. Drizzle the duck slices with plum sauce and pass extra sauce separately. Serve with saifun noodles or steamed white rice.

CHICKEN–SEASONED SAIFUN NOODLES

Serves 4

1   quart chicken stock (see page 167)

1   bunch green onions, finely chopped

1   tablespoon finely julienned fresh ginger

1   teaspoon soy sauce

1/8 teaspoon Asian sesame oil

1   package saifun noodles (approximately 6 ounces)

Bring the chicken stock to a boil in a medium saucepan. Add green onions, ginger, soy sauce and sesame oil. As soon as the mixture returns to a boil, add the saifun noodles and cook for approximately 3 minutes, or until the noodles are tender. Drain. Place the noodles on a plate and top with the Roast Duck in Plum Sauce.

FRENCH VANILLA ICE CREAM WITH CHOCOLATE, COFFEE AND LOGANBERRY TOPPING

Serves 4 to 6

In this recipe, I combine Whidbey's Loganberry Liqueur with semi-sweet chocolate and two Northwest favorites — espresso and fresh cherries — to create a decadently rich ice cream topping.

4   ounces semi-sweet chocolate chips

2   tablespoons Whidbey's Loganberry Liqueur

2   tablespoons espresso coffee, or 1 tablespoon instant espresso mixed with 2 tablespoons hot water

1   cup fresh Bing or Van cherries, pitted

French vanilla ice cream

Melt the chocolate in a double boiler over medium heat. Whisk in the liqueur and espresso until smooth. Fold in the cherries, mixing until smooth Serve warm over ice cream.

Suggested Wine
Merlot

Stocks and Sauces

VEAL STOCK

Makes approximately 1 quart

5 pounds veal bones

2 large yellow onions, quartered

4 stalks celery, cut into thirds

3 carrots, cut into thirds

3 shallots, halved

4 garlic cloves, peeled

2 bay leaves

4 whole peppercorns

2 tablespoons tomato paste

1/2 cup Chardonnay

4 quarts cold water

Preheat oven to 400°F. Place the veal bones, onions, celery, carrots, shallots and garlic in a large baking pan. Roast until the bones and vegetables are very brown, about 40 minutes, stirring occasionally.

Transfer the bones and vegetables to a 10-quart stock pot. Add the bay leaves, peppercorns, tomato paste, wine and water. Bring to a boil, skimming off the foam that develops on the top. Reduce heat to a simmer and cook, uncovered, for 6 hours. Strain the stock. Return the liquid to the heat and simmer until reduced by a third, about 1 hour. Place the stock in the refrigerator, uncovered, until cooled. Cover to store.

QUICK & SIMPLE FISH STOCK

Makes approximately 1 cup

2 cups shrimp or prawn shells

1/2 cup dry white wine

1/2 cup water

Simmer shells in water and wine for 15 minutes. Strain before using.

Chef's Tip

HOMEMADE STOCK

NOTHING REPLACES THE THICK, SILKY TEXTURE AND RICH FLAVOR OF HOMEMADE STOCKS. LEFTOVER STOCK CAN BE FROZEN IN ZIPPER–LOCK STORAGE BAGS FOR FUTURE USE.

VEGETABLE STOCK

Makes 2 to 3 quarts

3   celery stalks

1   yellow onion, cut in half

1   fennel bulb, cut in half

1   whole garlic bulb, sliced in half crosswise

2   carrots

3   sprigs fresh parsley

1   large tomato, cored and diced

2   bay leaves

6   whole black peppercorns

1   clove

1/2 cup Sauvignon Blanc or other dry white wine

1   tablespoon salt

6   quarts cold water

Combine all of the ingredients in a large pot. Bring to a boil over high heat. Reduce heat to a simmer and cook, uncovered, for 1 1/2 hours. Strain into a bowl. Cool, uncovered, in the refrigerator. Cover to store.

CHICKEN STOCK

Makes approximately 2 quarts

1   large stewing chicken or small whole fryer

4   quarts cold water

1   cup dry white wine

1   large yellow onion, cut in half

1   celery stalk, with leaves intact

3   sprigs fresh parsley

1   sprig fresh rosemary

3   garlic cloves, whole

3   whole peppercorns

1   bay leaf

3   tablespoons salt

Pinch of red pepper flakes

Combine all of the ingredients in a large, heavy stock pot. Bring the mixture to a boil over high heat. Reduce heat to a simmer, skimming off any foam that forms on the surface. Simmer the stock, uncovered, for 2 hours. Strain the stock and place in the refrigerator, uncovered, until cooled. Cover to store. Use within two days, or freeze.

SPICY ITALIAN SAUCE FOR GAME BIRDS

Makes 1 1/2 to 2 cups

Hunting wild game is still very popular in many parts of the Mediterranean, just as it is in the Pacific Northwest. I serve this thick, spicy sauce with roast quail, pheasant and other game birds.

1   cup Sauvignon Blanc

1   cup Cabernet Franc

3/4 cup red wine vinegar

1/4 cup balsamic vinegar

1/2 cup olive oil

1/4 cup shredded prosciutto

3   garlic cloves, peeled

2   large tomatoes, peeled, seeded and diced

1/2 lemon, peeled, seeded and thinly sliced

2   fresh sage leaves

2   sprigs fresh rosemary

4   juniper berries

2   chicken livers, finely chopped

4   anchovy fillets, finely chopped

Salt and freshly ground black pepper to taste

Combine the Sauvignon Blanc and Cabernet Franc in a nonreactive saucepan. Stir in the red wine vinegar, balsamic vinegar, olive oil, prosciutto, garlic, tomatoes, lemon slices, sage, rosemary and juniper berries. Bring the mixture to a boil over medium-high heat. Use a slotted spoon to remove the garlic, sage, rosemary and juniper berries. Stir in the chicken livers and anchovies. Reduce the heat to a brisk simmer and cook until the sauce is reduced by half, about 20 minutes. Season with salt and pepper.

Chef's Tip

ROASTING GAME BIRDS

TO PREPARE GAME BIRDS FOR ROASTING: COMBINE 1/4 CUP EXTRA-VIRGIN OLIVE OIL WITH 2 MINCED GARLIC CLOVES, SALT AND FRESHLY CRACKED BLACK PEPPER. RUB THE BIRDS INSIDE AND OUT WITH THIS MIXTURE, THEN COOK THEM ON A ROTISSERIE OR BARBECUE.

GINGER CHARDONNAY CREAM SAUCE WITH CAVIAR

Makes ²/₃ cup

*For a quick but very elegant touch, serve this gingery cream sauce over
spinach fettuccine, steamed mussels, roast chicken or steamed asparagus.*

1   tablespoon unsalted butter

1   tablespoon peanut oil

3   large shallots, finely diced

1   teaspoon grated fresh ginger

¼ cup Chardonnay

½ teaspoon grated lemon zest

1   cup whipping cream

Pinch of saffron threads

1   4-ounce jar caviar

Melt the butter with the peanut oil in a
saucepan over medium heat. Add the
shallots and ginger and cook until softened, about 5 minutes. Stir in the wine
and lemon zest and simmer for 2 minutes. Stir in the cream and saffron threads
and simmer until the sauce is thickened
and reduced by a third, about 12 minutes. Remove the sauce from the heat
and stir in the caviar. Serve warm.

Guide to Food and Wine Pairing

	Johannisberg Riesling	Gewurztraminer	Dry Riesling
	MEDIUM DRY		
MILD CHEESES	*	*	*
STRONGLY FLAVORED CHEESES			*
APPETIZERS	*	*	*
OYSTERS			
SHRIMP, CRAB, LOBSTER	*		*
CLAMS, MUSSELS			
SEAFOOD WITH WINE OR LIGHT SAUCES	*		*
SEAFOOD WITH CREAM SAUCES			
GRILLED FISH	*		*
SALMON			*
CREAM SAUCES			
MEDITERRANEAN–STYLE PASTA			
CHICKEN, TURKEY, GAME HEN	*	*	*
PHEASANT, DUCK, GOOSE		*	
ASIAN CUISINE	*	*	*
PORK, VEAL		*	*
LAMB			
GAME			
BEEF			
FRUIT AND LIGHT DESSERTS			
CHOCOLATE DESSERTS			

			RED WINES		DESSERT WINES				
	Sauvignon Blanc	Chardonnay	Syrah	Pinot Noir	Cabernet Franc	Merlot/Meritage	Cabernet Sauvignon	Late Harvest White Riesling	Late Harvest Semillon
Y			MEDIUM-BODIED		FULL-BODIED			SWEET	
	*								
	*	*	*	*	*	*	*	*	*
	*		*						
	*	*							
	*	*							
	*								
	*	*							
		*							
	*			*					
		*	*	*					
	*	*							
			*	*	*	*	*		
	*	*	*		*				
		*	*	*	*	*			
						*			
		*	*	*					
				*	*	*	*		
			*	*	*	*	*		
				*	*	*	*		
								*	*
						*	*		

Index

Adriatica Restaurant, 8, 26
Aged Cheeses and Fresh Fruit with Late Harvest White Riesling, 134, 139
Anchovy and Garlic Brussels Sprouts, 134, 138
Antipasto with Cabernet Vinaigrette, 144, 145
Appetizers
  Antipasto with Cabernet Vinaigrette, 145
  Calamari Fritti with Garlic Sauce, 28
  Caponata, 136
  Crab-Stuffed Endive, 52
  Dungeness Crab Spring Rolls, 69
  Figs, Prosciutto and Pecorino Cheese, 35
  Grilled Feta-Stuffed Grape Leaves, 135
  Marinated Mushrooms, 51
  Olive Tapenade, 39
  Smoked Chicken Crostini with Sun-Dried Tomato Paste and Roasted Garlic Mayonnaise, 149
Apple and Cabbage Slaw, 90, 91
Apple and Pear Sorbet, 144, 147
Apple and Prune Stuffed Pork Tenderloin, 74, 76
Apple Berry Cobbler with Hazelnut Crumble, 100, 103
Apple Strudel with Whidbey's Cream, 38, 41
Apples
  Aged Cheeses and Fresh Fruit with Late Harvest White Riesling, 139
  Apple and Cabbage Slaw, 91
  Apple and Pear Sorbet, 147
  Apple and Prune Stuffed Pork Tenderloin, 76
  Apple Berry Cobbler with Hazelnut Crumble, 103
  Apple Strudel with Whidbey's Cream, 41
  Baked Stuffed Apples with Late Harvest White Riesling, 99
  Poached Apples with Caramel Nut Topping, 25
Arugula with Olive Oil and Balsamic Vinaigrette, 128, 129
Asian Honey-Spiced Ribs, 96, 98
Asparagus
  Asparagus with Black Bean Sauce, 72
  Grilled Asparagus, 127
  Porcini and Asparagus Sauté, 33
  Warm Marinated Asparagus, 108
Asparagus with Black Bean Sauce, 68, 72

Baked Herbed Potatoes, 74, 77
Baked Stuffed Apples with Late Harvest White Riesling, 96, 99
Basil Prawn and Feta Pasta, 26, 29

Beans
  Hearty Chicken Bean Soup, 44
  Lamb and Bean Stew, 111
  Spicy Rice and Black Bean Salad, 23
  White Beans with Puttanesca Sauce, 114
Beef
  Asian Honey-Spiced Ribs, 98
  Braised Short Ribs in Cabernet Sauce, 146
  Cabernet Grilled Sirloin, 106
  Chopped Sirloin and Fresh Herb Burgers, 92
Berries
  Apple Berry Cobbler with Hazelnut Crumble, 103
  Cabbage and Cranberry Salad, 19
  Cherry Cranberry Chutney, 132
  Fall Root Crop Puree with Cherry Cranberry Chutney, 132
  Fresh Raspberry Puree with French Vanilla Ice Cream, 95
  Lemon Mousse with Strawberries and Whidbey's Whipped Cream, 55
  Peach Napoleon with Fresh Raspberries, 109
  Strawberry Trifle, 153
Bibb Lettuce and Dijon Salad, 26, 27
Blanc, Georges, 8
Braised Lamb Shanks, 86, 87
Braised Rabbit with Cherries, 140, 142
Braised Short Ribs in Cabernet Sauce, 144, 146
Breads. See Croatian Potato Bread
Broccoli with Pancetta, 74, 78
Brussels Sprouts. See Anchovy and Garlic Brussels Sprouts

Cabbage and Cranberry Salad, 18, 19
Cabernet Franc, 9, 81, 112, 124, 125, 128, 130, 135, 168
Cabernet Franc-Sage Sauce, 130
Cabernet Grilled Sirloin, 104, 106
Cabernet Sauvignon, 9, 10, 81, 90, 92, 100, 104, 105, 106, 111, 114, 135, 144, 145, 146, 160
Cabernet Vinaigrette, 145
Calamari Fritti with Garlic Sauce, 26, 28
Canoe Ridge Estate Winery, 8
Caponata, 134, 136
Caramel Nut Topping, 25
Chardonnay, 9, 10, 13, 18, 19, 30, 31, 36, 40, 43, 47, 54, 56, 62, 63, 166, 169
Chateau Ste. Michelle Winery, 6, 7, 8, 9, 22, 74, 115
Chenin Blanc, 13, 24

Cherries
   Braised Rabbit with Cherries, 142
   Fall Root Crop Puree with Cherry Cranberry
     Chutney, 132
   French Vanilla Ice Cream with Chocolate,
     Coffee and Loganberry Topping, 165
   Fresh Fruit in Late Harvest White Riesling, 159
   Quick Cherry Tart, 61
Cherry Cranberry Chutney, 132
Chicken
   Chicken Stock, 167
   Chicken-Seasoned Saifun Noodles, 164
   Croatian Kraut, Sausage and Chicken Stew, 40
   Hazelnut Chicken Breasts with Dijon Yogurt
     Sauce, 31
   Hearty Chicken Bean Soup, 44
   Italian Pounded Chicken, 36
   Mediterranean Couscous with Chicken, Lamb
     and Pork, 158
   Smoked Chicken and Spinach Salad, 75
   Smoked Chicken Crostini with Sun-Dried
     Tomato Paste and Roasted Garlic
     Mayonnaise, 149
   Smoked Chicken Lasagna, 113
   Spiedini Misti, 125
   Tuscan Chicken with Fresh Rosemary, 137
   Winter Chicken Pasta, 47
Chicken Stock, 167
Chicken-Seasoned Saifun Noodles, 160, 164
Child, Julia, 8
Chinese Barbecued Pork Roast, 68, 70
Chocolate, Coffee and Loganberry Topping, 165
Chopped Sirloin and Fresh Herb Burgers, 90, 92
Chutney
   Cherry Cranberry Chutney, 132
   Peach and Papaya Chutney, 58
Cornish Game Hens and Cabernet Franc-Sage
   Sauce, 128, 130
Couscous. See Mediterranean Couscous with
   Chicken, Lamb and Pork
Crab-Stuffed Endive, 50, 52
Creamy Garlic Potatoes, 104, 107
Crisp Romaine and Fresh Herb Salad, 140, 141
Croatian Kraut, Sausage and Chicken Stew, 38, 40
Croatian Potato Bread, 42, 43, 110
Croatian Spaghetti, 110, 112
Cucumbers
   Ginger Cucumber Salad, 162
   Mediterranean Salad, 157
   Poached Cucumbers and Tomato Salad, 53
Culinary Institute of America, 8

Dalmacija Ristoran, 8
Desserts
   Aged Cheeses and Fresh Fruit with Late Harvest
     White Riesling, 139
   Apple and Pear Sorbet, 147
   Apple Berry Cobbler with Hazelnut Crumble,
     103
   Apple Strudel with Whidbey's Cream, 41
   Baked Stuffed Apples with Late Harvest White
     Riesling, 99
   French Vanilla Ice Cream with Chocolate,
     Coffee and Loganberry Topping, 165
   Fresh Fruit in Late Harvest White Riesling, 159
   Fresh Raspberry Puree with French Vanilla Ice
     Cream, 95
   Hazelnut Plum Tart, 133
   Lemon Mousse with Strawberries and
     Whidbey's Whipped Cream, 55
   Lychee Nuts and Tangerines in White Riesling,
     73
   Peach Napoleon with Fresh Raspberries, 109
   Peach Pie, 65
   Poached Apples with Caramel Nut Topping, 25
   Poached Pears with Figs and Nuts, 123
   Quick Cherry Tart, 61
   Strawberry Trifle, 153
   Walnut Povitica, 79
Dijon Yogurt Sauce, 31
Dilled Peas in Butter Sauce, 86, 89
Disney Institute, 8
Dry Riesling, 13, 23, 38, 68, 70, 93, 161
Duck. See Roast Duck in Plum Sauce
Dungeness Crab Spring Rolls, 68, 69

Eggplant and Zucchini Strata, 34, 37

Fall Root Crop Puree, 128, 132
Figs
   Figs, Prosciutto and Pecorino Cheese, 35
   Marinated Fig and Prosciutto Salad, 105
   Poached Pears with Figs and Nuts, 123
   Figs, Prosciutto and Pecorino Cheese, 34, 35
Fish
   Fresh Spring Halibut Provençal with Poached
     Cucumbers and Tomato Salad, 53
   Halibut with Roasted Shallot-Pinot Sauce, 151
   Maple-Glazed Salmon with Peach and Papaya
     Chutney, 58
   Quick & Simple Fish Stock, 166
Flattened Potatoes, 118, 122
Fleur de Lis restaurant, 7
Food & Wine of the Pacific Northwest, 8

French Vanilla Ice Cream with Chocolate, Coffee and Loganberry Topping, 160, 165
Fresh Fruit in Late Harvest White Riesling, 156, 159
Fresh Greens and Garlic Sauté, 62, 64
Fresh Raspberry Puree with French Vanilla Ice Cream, 90, 95
Fresh Spring Halibut Provençal with Poached Cucumbers and Tomato Salad, 50, 53

Garden Salad, 148, 150
Garlic Sauce, 28
Garlic, Roasted, 107
Gewurztraminer, 13, 40
Ginger Chardonnay Cream Sauce with Caviar, 169
Ginger Cucumber Salad, 160, 162
Ginger Fried Rice, 71
Ginger-Merlot Sauce, 120
Ginger-Sesame Dipping Sauce, 69
Grilled Asparagus, 124, 127
Grilled Feta-Stuffed Grape Leaves, 134, 135
Grilled Garlic Basil Tomatoes, 118, 121
Grilled Marinated Pork Chops, 22, 24

Halibut with Roasted Shallot-Pinot Sauce, 148, 151
Hazelnut Chicken Breasts with Dijon Yogurt Sauce, 30, 31
Hazelnut Plum Tart, 128, 133
Hazelnuts, Toasted, 103
Hearty Chicken Bean Soup, 42, 44
Herbed New Potatoes, 148, 152
Herbs, 77

Italian Pounded Chicken, 34, 36

James Beard House, 8
Januik, Mike, 8
Johannisberg Riesling, 13, 22, 25, 51, 57, 74, 79

Lamb
    Braised Lamb Shanks, 87
    Lamb and Bean Stew, 111
    Lamb with Ginger-Merlot Sauce, 120
    Mediterranean Couscous with Chicken, Lamb and Pork, 158
    Spiedini Misti, 125
Lamb and Bean Stew, 110, 111
Lamb with Ginger-Merlot Sauce, 118, 120
Late Harvest White Riesling, 22, 25, 41, 56, 61, 62, 65, 74, 79, 99, 104, 109, 118, 123, 128, 133, 139, 144, 147, 148, 153, 156, 159
Lemon Mousse with Strawberries and Whidbey's Whipped Cream, 50, 55
Lentil Stew, 110, 115
Lychee Nuts and Tangerines in White Riesling, 68, 73

Manele Bay Hotel, 50
Maple-Glazed Salmon with Peach and Papaya Chutney, 56, 58
Marinated Fig and Prosciutto Salad, 104, 105

Marinated Mushrooms, 50, 51
Marinated Tomatoes, 38
Mediterranean Couscous with Chicken, Lamb and Pork, 156, 158
Mediterranean Salad, 156, 157
Meritage. See Red Meritage
Merlot, 9, 10, 81, 86, 87, 96, 98, 101, 115, 118, 120, 135, 142, 160, 163, 165
Mushrooms
    Marinated Mushrooms, 51
    Penne with Porcini Sauce, 101
    Porcini and Asparagus Sauté, 33
    Shiitake Mushroom Soup, 161
    Wild Rice and Porcini Pancakes, 54
    Wild Rice with Mushrooms and Herbs, 131

Northwest Wine Auction, 20

Old Country Potato Soup, 42, 46
Olive Tapenade, 38, 39
One-dish meals
    Croatian Kraut, Sausage and Chicken Stew, 40
    Croatian Spaghetti, 112
    Hearty Chicken Bean Soup, 44
    Lamb and Bean Stew, 111
    Lentil Stew, 115
    Old Country Potato Soup, 46
    Smoked Chicken Lasagna, 113
    Spicy Clam Pasta, 45
    White Beans with Puttanesca Sauce, 114
    Winter Chicken Pasta, 47
Onion. See Ultimate Baked Onion

Padovani, Philippe, 50
Pasta
    Basil Prawn and Feta Pasta, 29
    Croatian Spaghetti, 112
    Pasta and Prosciutto, 143
    Penne with Porcini Sauce, 101
    Smoked Chicken Lasagna, 113
    Spicy Clam Pasta, 45
    Winter Chicken Pasta, 47
Pasta al Dente, 29
Pasta and Prosciutto, 140, 143
Peach and Papaya Chutney, 58
Peach Napoleon with Fresh Raspberries, 104, 109
Peach Pie, 62, 65
Peaches
    Fresh Fruit in Late Harvest White Riesling, 159
    Peach and Papaya Chutney, 58
    Peach Napoleon with Fresh Raspberries, 109
    Peach Pie, 65
    Tomato-Peach Salsa, 94
Pears
    Aged Cheeses and Fresh Fruit with Late Harvest White Riesling, 139
    Apple and Pear Sorbet, 147
    Poached Pears with Figs and Nuts, 123

Peas. *See* Dilled Peas in Butter Sauce
Penne with Porcini Sauce, 100, 101
Peppers, Roasted, 39
Picardo, Tony, 81
Pinot Gris, 9, 13, 34, 35, 46
Pinot Noir, 9, 10, 81, 113, 148, 151, 152
Plums
    Fresh Fruit in Late Harvest White Riesling, 159
    Hazelnut Plum Tart, 133
    Roast Duck in Plum Sauce, 163
Poached Apples with Caramel Nut Topping, 22, 25
Poached Cucumbers and Tomato Salad, 53
Poached Pears with Figs and Nuts, 118, 123
Polenta with Roasted Garlic and Parmesan, 86, 88
Porcini and Asparagus Sauté, 30, 33
Pork
    Apple and Prune Stuffed Pork Tenderloin, 76
    Asian Honey-Spiced Ribs, 98
    Chinese Barbecued Pork Roast, 70
    Croatian Spaghetti, 112
    Grilled Marinated Pork Chops, 24
    Mediterranean Couscous with Chicken, Lamb
      and Pork, 158
    Spiedini Misti, 125
Potatoes
    Baked Herbed Potatoes, 77
    Creamy Garlic Potatoes, 107
    Croatian Potato Bread, 43
    Fall Root Crop Puree, 132
    Flattened Potatoes, 122
    Herbed New Potatoes, 152
    Old Country Potato Soup, 46
    Potatoes au Gratin, 32
    Warm Potato Salad, 97
Potatoes au Gratin, 30, 32
Poultry
    Cornish Game Hens and Cabernet Franc Sage
      Sauce, 130
    Roast Duck in Plum Sauce, 163
Puttanesca Sauce, 114

Quick & Simple Fish Stock, 166
Quick Cherry Tart, 56, 61
Quick Vegetable Stir-Fry, 56, 59

Rabbit. *See* Braised Rabbit with Cherries
Raffles Hotel, 118
Red Meritage, 81, 134, 135, 137, 140
Regent Hotel, 118
Rice
    Ginger Fried Rice, 71
    Saffron Rice, 126
    Spicy Rice and Black Bean Salad, 23
    Steamed Jasmine Rice, 60
    Wild Rice and Porcini Pancakes, 54
    Wild Rice with Mushrooms and Herbs, 131

Riesling, 9, 13, 22, 23, 25, 38, 41, 51, 56, 57, 61,
    62, 65, 68, 70, 73, 74, 79, 93, 95, 99, 104, 109,
    118, 123, 128, 133, 139, 144, 147, 148, 153,
    156, 159, 161
Ritz-Carlton Hotels, 8
Roast Duck in Plum Sauce, 160, 163
Roasted Garlic Mayonnaise, 149
Roasted Shallot-Pinot Sauce, 151
Romaine with Garlic Mustard Dressing, 118, 119

Saffron Rice, 124, 126
Salad dressings
    Cabernet Vinaigrette, 145
    Tarragon Dressing, 75
Salads
    Apple and Cabbage Slaw, 91
    Arugula with Olive Oil and Balsamic
      Vinaigrette, 129
    Bibb Lettuce and Dijon Salad, 27
    Cabbage and Cranberry Salad, 19
    Crisp Romaine and Fresh Herb Salad, 141
    Garden Salad, 150
    Ginger Cucumber Salad, 162
    Marinated Fig and Prosciutto Salad, 105
    Mediterranean Salad, 157
    Poached Cucumbers and Tomato Salad, 53
    Romaine with Garlic Mustard Dressing, 119
    Smoked Chicken and Spinach Salad, 75
    Spicy Rice and Black Bean Salad, 23
    Spinach and Scallop Salad, 57
    Warm Potato Salad, 97
Sam's Bar and Grill restaurant, 7
Sandy Lane Resort, 8
Sarich family, 6, 7, 11, 34, 38, 42, 45, 79, 81, 88,
    90, 96, 112, 144
Sauces
    Dijon Yogurt Sauce, 31
    Garlic Sauce, 28
    Ginger Chardonnay Cream Sauce with Caviar,
      169
    Ginger-Merlot Sauce, 120
    Ginger-Sesame Dipping Sauce, 69
    Puttanesca Sauce, 114
    Roasted Shallot-Pinot Sauce, 151
    Spicy Italian Sauce for Game Birds, 168
    Vanilla Custard Sauce, 109
Sausage
    Croatian Kraut, Sausage and Chicken Stew, 40
    Spiedini Misti, 125
Sauvignon Blanc, 9, 10, 13, 26, 29, 38, 40, 43, 44,
    45, 47, 50, 74, 76, 111, 143, 158, 167, 168
Seafood
    Basil Prawn and Feta Pasta, 29
    Calamari Fritti with Garlic Sauce, 28
    Crab-Stuffed Endive, 52
    Dungeness Crab Spring Rolls, 69
    Spicy Clam Pasta, 45
    Spinach and Scallop Salad, 57

Semillon, 9, 10, 13, 40, 68, 95, 118, 123, 161
Shallots, Roasted, 151
Shiitake Mushroom Soup, 160, 161
Smoked Chicken and Spinach Salad, 74, 75
Smoked Chicken Crostini with Sun-Dried Tomato
    Paste and Roasted Garlic Mayonnaise, 148, 149
Smoked Chicken Lasagna, 110, 113
Soups and Stews
    Croatian Kraut, Sausage and Chicken Stew, 40
    Hearty Chicken Bean Soup, 44
    Lamb and Bean Stew, 111
    Lentil Stew, 115
    Old Country Potato Soup, 46
    Shiitake Mushroom Soup, 161
Spicy Clam Pasta, 42, 45
Spicy Italian Sauce for Game Birds, 168
Spicy Pickled Green Tomatoes, 90, 93
Spicy Rice and Black Bean Salad, 22, 23
Spiedini Misti, 124, 125
Spinach
    Fresh Greens and Garlic Sauté, 64
    Smoked Chicken and Spinach Salad, 75
    Spinach and Scallop Salad, 57
    Spinach Sauté, 102
Spinach and Scallop Salad, 56, 57
Spinach Sauté, 100, 102
Squash Sticks, 18, 21
Stanford Court restaurant, 7
Steamed Jasmine Rice, 56, 60
Stocks
    Chicken Stock, 167
    Quick & Simple Fish Stock, 166
    Veal Stock, 166
    Vegetable Stock, 167
Strawberry Trifle, 148, 153
Sun-Dried Tomato Paste, 149
Swedish Culinary Olympic Team, 74
Syrah, 9, 81, 113, 156, 157

Tarragon Dressing, 75
Taste of the Northwest, 8, 140
Tomatoes
    Croatian Spaghetti, 112
    Grilled Garlic Basil Tomatoes, 121
    Mediterranean Salad, 157
    Poached Cucumbers and Tomato Salad, 53
    Puttanesca Sauce, 114
    Spicy Pickled Green Tomatoes, 93
    Sun-Dried Tomato Paste, 149
    Tomato-Peach Salsa, 94
Tomato-Peach Salsa, 90, 94
Tranquilli, Joey, 45
Tuscan Chicken with Fresh Rosemary, 134, 137

Ultimate Baked Onion, 18, 20

Vanilla Custard Sauce, 109

Veal
    Veal Loin with Sweet Pepper Puree, 63
    Veal Stock, 166
Veal Loin with Sweet Pepper Puree, 62, 63
Veal Stock, 166
Vegetable dishes
    Anchovy and Garlic Brussels Sprouts, 138
    Asparagus with Black Bean Sauce, 72
    Baked Herbed Potatoes, 77
    Broccoli with Pancetta, 78
    Creamy Garlic Potatoes, 107
    Dilled Peas in Butter Sauce, 89
    Eggplant and Zucchini Strata, 37
    Fall Root Crop Puree, 132
    Flattened Potatoes, 122
    Fresh Greens and Garlic Sauté, 64
    Grilled Asparagus, 127
    Grilled Garlic Basil Tomatoes, 121
    Herbed New Potatoes, 152
    Porcini and Asparagus Sauté, 33
    Potatoes au Gratin, 32
    Quick Vegetable Stir-Fry, 59
    Spinach Sauté, 102
    Squash Sticks, 21
    Warm Marinated Asparagus, 108
    Vegetable Stock, 167
Vegetarian
    Eggplant and Zucchini Strata, 37
    Lentil Stew, 115
    White Beans with Puttanesca Sauce, 114

Walnut Povitica, 74, 79
Warm Marinated Asparagus, 104, 108
Warm Potato Salad, 96, 97
Whidbey's Cream, 41
Whidbey's Whipped Cream, 55
White Beans with Puttanesca Sauce, 110, 114
Wild Rice and Porcini Pancakes, 50, 54
Wild Rice with Mushrooms and Herbs, 128, 131
Wine
    aging, 88
    aroma, 129
    balance, 75
    barrel aging, 33
    breathing and decanting, 119
    cooking with, 70
    food and wine pairing, 141
    glasses, 143
    late harvest, 95
    sensual pleasures of, 131
    serving dessert, 65
    serving temperature, 102
    storing, 54
    tannin, 138
    vintage dates, 78
    with vinegar and citrus, 51
Winter Chicken Pasta, 42, 47
Wong, Alan, 8